ALSO BY NIGEL & MAGGIE PERCY

Learn Dowsing: Your Natural Psychic Power

The Busy Person's Guide To Energy Clearing

The Busy Person's Guide To Space Clearing

The Busy Person's Guide To Ghosts, Curses & Aliens

The Busy Person's Guide: The Complete Series on Energy Clearing

The Nature Of Intuition: Understand & Harness Your Intuitive Ability

Pendulums for Guidance & Healing

Dowsing For Health: Awaken Your Hidden Talent

Caring For Your Animal Companion: The Intuitive, Natural Way To A Happy, Healthy Pet

Dowsing Ethics: Replacing Intentions With Integrity

Dowsing: Practical Enlightenment

The Dowsing State: Secret Key To Accurate Dowsing

Ask The Right Question: The Essential Sourcebook Of Good Dowsing Questions

101 Amazing Things You Can Do With Dowsing

The Essence Of Dowsing by Nigel Percy

The Credibility Of Dowsing, edited by Nigel Percy

Healing Made Simple: Change Your Mind & Improve Your Health

Dowsing Reference Library

THE DOWSING
ENCYCLOPEDIA

NIGEL PERCY

MAGGIE PERCY

ISBN: 978-0-9978816-4-6 (Ebook version)

ISBN: 978-1-946014-39-9 (Paperback version)

Sixth Sense Books

150 Buck Run E

Dahlonega, GA 30533

Email address: discoveringdowsing@gmail.com

CONTENTS

ACKNOWLEDGMENTS

We want to thank the Sixth Sense Books community for help in the publication of this book. The support of our tribe makes it possible for us to publish our books, allowing us to reach the largest possible audience worldwide. During the crowdfunding campaign before the publication of this book in January 2016, we received generous donations from readers in 8 countries: the U.S., Canada, the U.K., Australia, New Zealand, Italy, Brazil and Thailand.

A special shout of thanks goes out to: Deborah Cerar, Ana Maria Vasquez, Roy Dickson, Amelie St. Pierre, Ashraf Verjee, Julia Marks, Donna Kossar, Mary Ellen & Kevin Hale, Phyllis Baumann, Sue Miller, Debbie Thrasher, Liz Sokoski, Sheila Green, Susana Gama, Cynthia Garbarsky, Lori Murray, Glenda Spiwak, J. Darrell, Elizabeth Strothman, Jayne Robbins, Antonio Bortolotti and Michele Fitzgerald.

INTRODUCTION

Encyclopedias are often the result of a large team of writers, researchers, editors, editors-in-chief, and subject specialists who have a reasonably large budget and access to a wide variety of off-line sources such as specialist libraries. This encyclopedia, however, is the result only of my efforts. To be more accurate, I have written the articles and done the research but I did it consulting with and listening to my wife, Maggie. So, if there is to be any blame laid anywhere, it should come squarely at me. I cannot fob it off to some unnamed, underpaid researcher. It's all me. Which is a good thing, as far as I can see.

Any encyclopedia which purports to encompass a subject is, invariably, out of date pretty much as soon as it is published. This might happen to this volume. But I think it less prone to being out-of-date mainly due to the way I have selected which articles to add and which to leave out, as I explain below.

Although it is the result of my own thoughts, research and efforts, I have tried to maintain, as far as I can manage, a dispassionate approach to the whole subject. Having been a dowser for over thirty years, however, there will be traceable amounts of personal bias in some of the articles. I have diligently sought to eradicate the obvious ones, but for those which remain, I crave your indulgence and promise to improve when, and if, I update this.

The main reason it was attempted was that both myself and Maggie, my wife and also an excellent long-time dowser, were concerned that the teaching of dowsing was leaving out a lot of what we considered to be essential elements. For example, the idea of the dowsing state is usually, at this time, completely ignored in favor of getting the dowsing tool to move after a cursory glance at developing good questions. In other words, dowsing is being seen as a quick and easy tool but without any substance to it. Frequently people who have been 'taught' to dowse leave with little or no idea how they can apply it in their lives and either lose interest or develop exceedingly bad habits because there is no-one to tell them otherwise.

Added to this was the realization that dowsing, by and large, is grossly misunderstood. For many people, the only connection they have with dowsing is of water dowsing. It is by far the most common association. But, beyond this, many dowsers themselves confuse dowsing with healing or intention. If it is growing in popularity then it is to the detriment of understanding what dowsing really entails. And it was in order to offset these skewed conceptions that this encyclopedia was started.

To put it another way; the great strength of dowsing is that it is easy to learn, and the great weakness of dowsing is that it is easy to learn. Learning it is one thing, using and understanding it is another thing entirely. If, therefore, there is one sole purpose behind this present work, it is the wish that, through perusing it, a clear and concise picture of what dowsing actually is will be made plain. Misconceptions, misunderstandings (both deliberate and accidental) and ignorance will, it is hoped, be swept away or dispersed. In their place will develop a greater appreciation of this innate human skill and how *useful* in all aspects of life it can be when applied well.

As I mentioned earlier, any such work can never claim to be complete and all-embracing. There will always be something left out or unexplained.

Given that state of affairs, I should like to explain what is and what is not to be found inside these pages.

Firstly, I have tried to include all the major tools, techniques and methods both Maggie and I have come across in our years of learning, applying and teaching dowsing. Therefore, you will find entries for the obvious and popular pendulum, but also for others such as the less-recognized Mager Rosette, a flexible and interesting adjunct to any dowser's repertoire.

I have also tried to demystify some of the more commonly heard terms used in dowsing in the (admittedly) vain and (probably) futile hope that some clarity will spread throughout the dowsing community. Even if that does not occur, then at least there will be this volume which might help settle some arguments between two friendly dowsers now and then.

Additionally, I have sought to provide a wider background to dowsing than just terms, tools and techniques by including some articles on the broader aspects of the skill. Areas such as skepticism, or the origin of the word itself, some of the more common fallacies associated with dowsing and a very brief sketch of the history of the subject are amongst such examples.

The overall plan, therefore, was to provide a well-rounded and detailed examination of this wonderful, natural human skill such that the seasoned dowser as well as the newcomer or the interested bystander could derive some use from it and gain in their understanding by being able to gather an oversight which is, presently, unavailable elsewhere. I have sought, wherever possible, to provide references to facts stated. In many cases, a reasonably focused search on the web was all that was necessary. But, in a few cases, I have referenced a particular website for providing somewhat arcane or unusual information not otherwise reasonably accessible to the casual searcher.

I have refrained from listing all the various volumes I have used for no good reason other than that, if you, dear reader, are really interested in this subject, then a good deal of fun and insight can be gained from tracking down good, reliable sources to use for yourself. Do be aware, however, that just because a website or two repeat certain information does not mean it is reliable. The internet is a wonderful way to proliferate information without ever checking it or even acknowledging that it was copied wholesale elsewhere. Plagiarism is rife!

Therefore, in many cases, assumptions which have a wide following have been singularly difficult to track down to their source. What has surprised me in doing this research is how difficult it is to pin down an idea, a term, or a concept about dowsing to a definite and precise source. Many times I have started on what seemed an easily identifiable idea only to discover that its origins were confused to begin with, made worse over time (often in all innocence), before entering into what presently seems to be a static meaning, but which has little connection with the past.

In following such confusing trails, it is highly likely that I have made errors. Where possible, I have sought to acknowledge the confusion, but am willing to accept that something else could be added to (or removed from) the entry to make it more accurate. I would be obliged, therefore, if any reader can add to this volume by providing precise references to new sources, or providing corrections (again with references) to assumptions or ideas made here. I am not interested in hearing from those I have upset with what I have written unless and until any such refutation can be accompanied by some diligent, pertinent and appropriate references (which would *not* include personal preferences, ideas or theories). If any such entries do upset you in some fashion, I apologize and look forward to your detailed correction. (See also the last sentence of this introduction.)

One of the chief problems with books on dowsing in general, by and large that is, is that they tend to expound on the author's viewpoint, technique or beliefs to the exclusion of everything else. While this is perfectly justified and to be expected, it does have drawbacks. In general, it means that there are a great variety of confusing, and often conflicting, theories around about how dowsing works or the 'right' way to use a tool, or the 'proper' technique to be used. There is little to judge any of them against, apart from whether such ideas and theories attract the reader or not.

Therefore, I have studiously avoided coming down heavily in favor of one set of ideas over another. Instead, I have striven to create a balanced approach to the many possible views on dowsing in the hope that the reader will be in a better position to make an informed choice as to which is the more coherent set of beliefs within which to use dowsing.

I have, however, been at pains to point out where sloppy thinking or rash assumptions have contributed to an idea, an approach, or a theory associated with dowsing. Just because it is a hobby to many people does not mean that it should be excused some careful thought. It would be like a weekend woodworker not paying any attention to the care of the tools used. If something is to be done, and to be done as well as possible by each individual (or what's the point of doing anything?), then it deserves to be done with some thought and consideration, not in a haphazard fashion with little care for the consequences.

I have chosen, quite deliberately, to omit certain entries which would normally be expected by those who have been dowsing for some time. These include biographies or theories of existing or very recently deceased dowsers, however well-known they might be amongst various groups. I have omitted them for the simple reason that I do not believe it is possible, this close to them, to be able to make adequate judgments as to the value or otherwise of their contributions to the dowsing arena. Some might have oblique mentions, but are nowhere central to any entry.

I have also chosen to exclude all such entries which are not directly related to dowsing, but are often considered as part of the dowser's arsenal of understanding. This collection includes the vast majority of terms used in earth energy dowsing. You will not find the various proposed earth grids and the like discussed in detail here, nor is there discussion of the supposed effects such energies might have on people. That is not dowsing related; that is health related instead. Ley lines, however, for example, do get an entry to themselves because they are frequent causes of confusion amongst dowsers.

Equally, and obviously to some dowsers, there is nothing about healing techniques. Dowsing and healing are firm partners in many peoples' minds. And rightly so. One most certainly complements the other to a great degree. However, there is a widespread lack of understanding that they are completely different beasts. Therefore, by focusing only on dowsing, I hope, by the omission of talk of healing, to be able to allow readers a clearer understanding of the difference between these two; by bringing dowsing into clear and sharp relief rather than adding to any existing muddle and discussing the two together.

One other huge problem exists within the current perception of dowsing, and it is one which spreads like wildfire, and it is down, in most cases, to either poor teaching or weak thinking, probably both. It is the confusion and muddle which exists between the use of dowsing and the use of intention. Very often, either in books, on the web, in presentations or in social media groups, someone will speak of an action, such as healing or some such thing, and state that by swinging the pendulum or other tool, the effect was achieved.

It should be stated boldly and loudly in large letters that moving the tool does not imply dowsing. And that focusing on an outcome is not dowsing, but intention. The confusion persists and only acts to further cloud the general understanding of what exactly this remarkable skill actually consists of; the ability to gain answers to specific questions which are not available to the rational mind.

Finally, I have not included an area which is a personal favorite of mine; the use of dowsing in personal growth. I have written about the importance of dowsing in this area, but have restrained myself from going into details about the various personal growth techniques which use dowsing to one degree or another. Additionally, there are so many techniques and routes one can take towards self-improvement, but some are not, in and of themselves, anything to do with dowsing. They are, in virtually every case, susceptible to the help dowsing can give in terms of refinement and focus, but dowsing *per se* is not central to their efficacy.

One additional point I would like to make is that it is my wish that, with this present volume, it is made clear just how interesting, useful and complex dowsing actually is. And that this complexity is what makes it such a valuable tool which can be used by anyone, if they will simply take the time to master the basics. Too many people misunderstand dowsing and what it is, as well as what it can be used for. By presenting the various aspects of the subject in, I hope, a clear and cogent fashion, I earnestly hope that more and more people will be drawn to taking it up for themselves and, beyond that, use it to inquire into and improve their lives.

It would be useful to state as clearly as possible what dowsing is, or how it might be considered as something of value in its own right. That understanding might be garnered by paying close attention throughout the encyclopedia, but it makes more sense to state it here. Dowsing is often defined by how it is used or applied, or the tools associated with it. While that might be of use, it leaves out so much. For dowsing is not just how you use it, but it is also about the state of mind necessary for it to happen. As such, it is very much a mental thing. But it is a mental thing which encourages intuition. Therefore it is, as one writer has described it, 'a paradoxical mental tool! A useful one, though, for it fits neatly into the awkward gap between the 'thinking' tools of logic, analysis and 'scientific method', and the 'feeling' tools of imagination, intuition and 'subjective meaning'.' (Tom Graves, *Dowsing Techniques and Applications*, Turnstone Books, 1976 p.12)

It is a personal thing. It is individual, as each person who dowses will develop his or her own protocols and techniques. It is not, despite the vociferous claims of some, a tool to change the world. But it can safely be considered to be a tool to change yourself. It is not what you do with it as much as it what it does with you. Analysis, intuition, awareness, understanding, personal growth: these are all the province of dowsing. The tools and the techniques and the applications are merely the external signs, the outward representations of this most personal and entirely natural skill. It is a skill to which we all have access, which anyone can learn and everyone can use to their own benefit.

This volume deals with some of the traditional ideas in dowsing including some of the new thoughts filtering in as well as reviving some of the older ideas and concepts. What you choose to take away for yourself will, of course, be up to you. If nothing else, one or more of the entries here might inspire your to dowse more frequently or use a different technique, or even think in a new way. If it makes any change in you, your perception or ideas, then it will have served its purpose.

And, finally, if you come across something which enrages you because it goes against everything you hold dear, then please try to remember what Aristotle once said, "It is the mark of an educated mind to be able to entertain a thought without accepting it."

Nigel Percy

March 2016

HOW TO USE THIS BOOK

Depending on your own preferences, you may wish to open this volume up to an entry dear to your heart, or you might just dip here and there. It may be that you have arrived at this page by accident, or only after having read everything else of interest first.

If I might suggest an alternative approach, it would be that, first, you read the introduction. Some people are naturally averse to such things, thinking that they are the place where the author rambles on about his thought processes or how it all came about. I admit there is a smidgeon of that in the introduction, but do not pass it by for that reason.

Instead, peruse it for the real meat which is there; an explanation of why such a book is needed in this day and age. Once you have that under your belt, so to speak (and for a useful and necessary definition of dowsing), then come back here and briefly acquaint yourself with how to find your way around the rest of it.

If there is a reference in the entry to another entry elsewhere, it is referenced thus:

Blink dowsing is a type of deviceless dowsing (q.v.). Refer to the entry 'Deviceless Dowsing' for more detail.

Where it is thought that additional information would be useful, but there is no direct reference to it in the entry itself, then the reader is directed to it as in the following example:

(See DIVINATION, RHABDOMANCY)

In the above case, two other entries are indicated.

I would also like to urge you to use this book to expand your ideas, to develop and extend your thinking as well as improve your dowsing by introducing you to new ways of looking at and, above all, using this skill. Therefore, take the time to seek out and read those entries which either intrigue you the most, or outrage you the most. In either case, you will probably learn something you had not bargained for.

Only then would I suggest reading those entries the titles of which are familiar to you, because you will then be in the right frame of mind to see those in new ways as well.

Above all, happy dowsing!

A

Accuracy

Accuracy is one of the biggest challenges which faces dowsers. Accuracy is usually interpreted to mean, 'Was the answer provided by dowsing proven to be correct?'

Obviously, it makes no sense to speak of accuracy when dowsing intangible questions, targets which cannot be verified. To understand accuracy, it is necessary to work on aspects which can be verified, either by seeing results turn out as forecasted, or by another person verifying the answer.

Although there is no hard and fast evidence on this subject, anecdotally it appears that, when beginning dowsing, the success rate is usually quite high. After a period of time, however, which varies from dowser to dowser, the accuracy rate falls off before settling at what seems to be a constant.

Whether this is due to faith or belief in oneself at first, or the fact that there is nothing blocking the ability, no pre-conceived beliefs if you will, new dowsers tend to report a high success factor. It may also be due to the dowser being drawn initially to an area of dowsing in which competence is most easily seen, thereby providing positive feedback and increasing the satisfaction found in dowsing. A smaller number of dowsing attempts could give a skewed idea of accuracy.

The lowering of accuracy might also be due to the fact that dowsing is tried out on a wider range of subjects at first, some of which the dowser is less competent at than others. It might also be due to other beliefs (q.v.) or new ideas acting as methods of questioning oneself acting as barriers to a simple acceptance of the skill being applied.

Being able to discover which area or areas are strengths in dowsing will help to keep the accuracy high. As an example, many water dowsers, who often do very little of anything else, can have success rates of 95% and above. As an aside, nobody who is honest has ever claimed 100% accuracy in tangible target dowsing, the only sort of dowsing which can be objectively measured.

That being said, accuracy can certainly be improved by taking some simple steps. Each of the following steps addresses one of the three states: mental, emotional and physical. Each of these, ideally, should be considered in turn prior to dowsing in order to boost your accuracy.

The first, and biggest block to accuracy is the question one asks prior to dowsing. (See QUESTIONS) This is the mental aspect.

The second block is not being in the Dowsing State (q.v.) when dowsing the question. This comprises the emotional aspect.

The third area which can contribute to problems are physiological issues. First amongst these is the state of hydration (q.v.). Being inadequately hydrated usually leads to dowsing errors. Although the physiological reasons have not been fully explored by any independent study, it would seem that a lack of water in the body inhibits the dowsing response, making it slower, weaker, non-existent or flipped (see POLARITY and SWITCHING).

≈

Agricola

Agricola (Georgius Agricola) was the Latinized name of Georg Bauer, who lived in Germany during the 16th Century and who wrote a book cataloguing the art of finding, mining, refining and smelting minerals. The book was titled *De Re Metallica* (On The Nature of Metals) and was published in 1556, one year after his death. The delay was due to assembling the various woodcuts for illustrations for the text.

The book proved to be immensely popular and remained as a standard text on mining for over a century. An interesting side note is that the first English translation appeared in 1912, with one of the principal translators being the future President of the USA, Herbert Hoover, who at the time was a mining engineer.

The reason Agricola's name is associated with dowsing is because of the appearance of a woodcut in the volume which clearly shows for the first time, the use of dowsing to locate minerals. In the woodcut (shown below), a dowser is to be seen selecting and cutting a rod from a tree in the background, then walking with it pointing up and finally with the rod pointing down at the location of the mineral.

Prior to this publication, there had not been specific, illustrated references to dowsing and to dowsing rods. Agricola's work was the clearest indication of how dowsing was widely used by German miners as a practical technique. This single illustration is the one most frequently used to illustrate the history of dowsing (q.v.) as well as being proof (along with the detailed text) that dowsing was a skill which actually worked for a section of the population.

German miners were thought to be responsible for bringing dowsing into England a little later on, during the reign of Elizabeth I (1558 -1603). It was widely thought that they were the most skillful of miners and that skill was, in part, attributed to their use of dowsing. But it is this illustration, in Agricola's book, which remains as probably the single most famous historical representation of dowsing, and hence is the one aspect of his work which remains as a reference today.

〜

ARCHEOLOGICAL DOWSING

Archeological dowsing is a type of dowsing which aims to explore, map or discover sites of historical interest without disturbing the ground.

Obviously, having said that, the only way of proving any result would be to actually dig. This, however, is a highly specialized skill and should never be undertaken by any dowser if there is the least concern that there is a site of interest. Some dowsers use the skill to look for old coins (see TREASURE DOWSING). If the dowsing result suggests that there is something small and isolated, it would still be advisable to investigate it as carefully as possible, making sure a complete and thorough record is made to show to any interested parties later on.

One of the main uses of this type of dowsing is to explore a large site and to isolate specific areas as being the most worthy of investigation. That, of course, would require an archeologist to state what is meant, in the context of the site, as being of importance. And here the major problem lies, for there are few if any, professional archeologists who would be willing to allow any dowser, no matter how skilled, to survey a site and suggest which areas are which. To do so would invite the archeologist to be ridiculed as a gullible fool by his peers.

Of course, there will always be the occasional opportunity where a dowser might be invited to exercise his or her skill in such areas.

It also possible to use dowsing to explore, map and record or measure an area and then to use historical sources to help confirm or deny what was dowsed. This would involve looking at old maps, reading old documents and the like to help gain a picture of the place as dowsed.

Some dowsers certainly seem to exhibit a skill in this area, being able to state where walls were, where roads or paths were, even the type of construction used in some cases. In a few cases, their results have been verified.

The reason many dowser might fail to be successful at this type of dowsing would be because of the skepticism (q.v.) of those present.

∼

ARMY, **Dowsing Used By**

The use of dowsing by the armed forces is something which is generally known and accepted as we approach the present. The further back we go, the less certainty there is. For example, it is widely reported in many books and articles online that, during the Gallipoli campaign in the First World War, a dowser was able to discover a source of water which was much needed by the troops who were there. This is probably the first case where it has been verified, although few who refer to it have spent the time to do so.

In this case, the dowser was a man named William Dawkins. A biography of William Dawkins was self-published by Judith Ingle in 1995 containing his letters and extracts from his diary. The book, however, is difficult to obtain. The only other real reference found so far is that of the newsletter of the Dowsing Society of Victoria's newsletter where an article originally posted in the British Society of Dowser's Newsletter of 2006 is republished, albeit with a part of it missing. In this, it speaks of the original author ended up speaking with someone who was adopted by William's mother who, in turn, used to read the letters and the use of dowsing was, therefore, common knowledge.

Even so, the precise details, how much water was obtained and where, is still vague or uncertain at best. Nevertheless, it is hard to prove the use of dowsing by armed forces, beyond conjecture and supposition, much earlier than this. In fact, much of what appears to be proof on the internet of how dowsing is used by the military is merely copying and rewording of an alleged reference from one place to another, ending up in a cycle of repetition which, because it is continuously repeated, is taken as truth (q.v.).

And that is usually because the authors really want such proof (q.v.) to exist.

From this time forward, however, the spread of knowledge about dowsing and how it is used by the military, is much easier to access. General Patton's use of a dowser in the Libyan desert in World War Two is seemingly well-documented, although the actual proof is still in need of being more obvious. But, in the Vietnamese conflict, dowsing was taught to

Marines by Louis Matacia, a surveyor whose hobby was dowsing, to help them locate tunnels where the enemy were hiding and other useful techniques for survival. This is very well-documented.

Also, the Royal Corps of Engineers were taught the rudiments of dowsing at Sandhurst and Colonel Harry Grattan, CBE, Royal Engineers, located the water for the HQ of the British Army on the Rhine in 1952.

In other countries, there is much implication of the use of dowsing by military forces, but carefully researched facts are hard to come by. Doubtless there are many small, privately printed and well-researched publications which do give details of these, and the interested reader is urged to find them and bring them to light for the better clarification and understanding of how this technique is applied in these areas.

In summary, however, it is clear that, given the information which is readily available, together with the amount of circumstantial evidence and stories, dowsing is a technique which is readily applied by members of the armed forces around the world for various reasons; from helping their own side, to locating the enemy or some aspect of they opposing forces.

To assume that all military uses are valueless or only carried out by irregular individuals without sanction, is to misread the situation and all available evidence which points firmly to the contrary.

∽

AURAMETER

An aurameter is a type of dowsing tool (q.v.). It was apparently designed by a Californian dowser, Verne Cameron, in the middle of the 20th century. In a sense, it can be compared to an L-rod (q.v.) with springs.

The tool has a wire coming from the handle which has several turns in it, making a spring. The last section of wire is then angled and has a weight attached. In the ready position, the weighted tip is held pointed upwards. The idea is that the weighted point at the end is made more sensitive to slight movements of the dowser because of the spring and the angle at which the end weight is held.

The tool got its name from the intended use it was put to, that of outlining, or identifying the human aura and finding any areas of weakness or other problems there. Of course, as with any dowsing tool, the aurameter can also be used for other purposes, but it is chiefly used for following energy fields or lines.

Its construction means that it places less stress on the dowser than most other tools. However, you do need to get used to it and they do tend to be at the more expensive end of dowsing tools.

∼

Autoscope

An autoscope is the name given by Professor Barrett (*The Credibility of Dowsing*), to any instrument which allows involuntary movements to occur. The term itself means 'self viewer' and, in terms of dowsing tools, is useful, as it does allow the person to 'see' his or her's reactions.

The term has since fallen out of fashion, but is useful to remember as a means of reminding oneself that any reaction of a tool in dowsing is just one's own reaction and nothing else.

∼

AYMAR

Jacques Aymar, born in 1662 in France, is often upheld as a wonderful example of the use of dowsing in the non-physical realm. Principally, he is offered as the first well-documented story of dowsing being used in the moral field; to pursue and find criminals.

The story most closely associated with him concerns the murder of Antoine Boubon Savetier and his wife in Lyons in July of 1692. They owned a wine shop and had both been bludgeoned to death with a billhook and been robbed of about 500 livres (a goodly amount in those days). The authorities made little progress and eventually Aymar was called upon to help them.

The reason for this was that he had, in 1688, firstly discovered the body of a murdered woman and then subsequently identified the widower as the murderer, which was proven when he immediately tried to flee. Therefore, Aymar had established his ability in such matters.

However, the authorities were not gullible and tested him first by burying the murder weapon amongst similar tools and challenged him to find the location and the correct tool. This he did.

Convinced that he was capable of then finding the murderer or murderers, he was given temporary legal powers and proceeded to track the culprits. During this process, he declared that there had been three people involved and identified the places they stopped and drank.

Eventually he led the authorities to a jail in a different town where he singled out one youth who had just been arrested for larceny. He was easily identifiable due to a hunchback and was identified by witnesses back at Lyons and the youth confessed. The youth named the other two accomplices and they were tracked by Aymar as heading towards Genoa, over which there was no jurisdiction. At which point, the chase was abandoned.

This case made Aymar a celebrity and he was invited to demonstrate his abilities by the Prince de Condé the following year. Although he was successful in some of the tests, he performed less well than expected and his credibility was damaged.

However, he did not stop using his dowsing in the moral sphere, whilst also using it to locate water and minerals. He used his dowsing for the Catholics during the Revolt of the Camisards (1702-1705: a protestant uprising in south-central France against long-term persecution by the Catholics). He identified, with his dowsing, those who were Huguenots (protestants), who were later executed. Note that this took place after the Holy Inquisition's decree against the use of dowsing in criminal proceedings. (See RELIGION AND DOWSING)

The story of Aymar, as noted, is frequently offered as an example of how dowsing might be used other than in the location of physical objects or underground water or minerals. His abilities were carefully documented.

But, as with many dowsers, there are also the failures which are inexplicable. Chief amongst them was his failure to identify a murder site in Paris when tested by Condé in 1693.

Aymar's story, then, is important, not necessarily for the tracing of criminals, although that is remarkable, but for the ethical dilemmas which arise when dowsing is used in the moral sphere. For example, another dowser (unnamed) was followed by a large and jeering crowd as he pointed out the houses of married women who had committed adultery.

The authorities, both civil and religious, entered into serious debate about the admissibility of any evidence obtained in such a manner. It is not surprising that the decree (noted above) was issued nine years after Aymar's exploits, and the civil authorities followed a similar approach.

(See ETHICS)

B

Baubiologie

Other terms for this area of study are Building Biology or Geobiology. The term Baubiologie (building biology) is the preferred term in this reference work because the study has its origins in Germany and that is the term most widely used in Europe.

The reason for including this is that dowsing is an integral part of the process.

There are 25 principles of this area of study which are used to evaluate and help create and maintain a healthy environment to live in. They are listed on the website of the International Institute of Bau-Biologie and Ecology (IBE), founded 1987. The relevant ones for the purposes of this volume are as follows:

- The Earth's natural magnetic field shall not be altered or distorted.
- Man-made electromagnetic radiation shall be eliminated (or reduced as much as possible)….
- Cosmic and terrestrial radiation is essential and shall be interfered with as little as possible.

- Harmonic measures, proportions and shapes need to be taken into consideration.

These are areas where the practice of space clearing (q.v.) overlaps. In baubiologie, however, the emphasis is more on the balancing of the various aspects of the environment.

A baubiologist will frequently use dowsing to investigate the unseen aspects of the environment

∼

BEAUSOLEIL, Baron & Baronness de

Jean du Chatelet, Baron du Beausoleil and Auffembach (1578 - c.1645) married Martine Bertereau (c.1600 - c.1642) in 1610. He was a mining expert and she was the daughter of French mine owners. Without entering into all the details, the main points of their story are as follows.

They became expert at locating and opening up mines and were given commissions to do so in France. However, they were not paid. Their exploits in France were in two parts. The first ended when they were accused of sorcery and fled the country. The second ended in their arrest and separate imprisonment; he in the Bastille and she and one of their daughters in the state prison of Vincennes. They never received a trial and died in those places. Their work had taken place over 40 years and they had identified a remarkable number of mines, with the intention that France would gain independence in mineral wealth by exploiting her own natural resources.

Their imprisonment was due to the revival of charges of magic and sorcery mainly due to the use of dowsing rods to locate the ores to be mined. Apparently Martine had about seven different types of rods which she used in her work.

Although this is, without doubt, a sorry tale, it also shows that systematic use of dowsing over many years did develop an industry, or, at least, give opportunity for it to be developed.

Also of interest is that Martine is one of the first women to be associated with dowsing in any professional context, and also is one of the best.

∿

Beliefs

The use of dowsing to examine or access beliefs is an area which has been developing rapidly over the last several years.

In this case, the beliefs referred to are those held in the subconscious (q.v.). The beliefs we consciously have are obvious and accessible to simple inquiry. However, the beliefs held in the subconscious are less accessible.

It is becoming more widely accepted (by those in personal development work) that subconscious beliefs are responsible for many of the issues and conflicts which can and do occur in our personal lives. They are also held to be partly responsible for setting up blocks to our goals and maintaining them in the face of other personal growth techniques. Therefore, addressing them directly has become another important tool in the arsenal of those who wish to achieve personal growth. (See PERSONAL GROWTH)

Dowsing, the skill of acquiring information not available to the rational mind, is a perfect tool with which to examine and explore the subconscious. Using dowsing, it is possible to discover what beliefs there might be in the subconscious which might be blocking one's progress. And, once known, they can be dealt with using a variety of methods or therapies.

It is beyond the scope of this present volume to detail how such beliefs may be discovered using dowsing, but it is important to realize that dowsing is a superb tool for directly accessing the subconscious. Indeed, it might be argued that this use of dowsing is the single most potent application of the skill.

One other aspect of beliefs is worth mentioning as well. Everyone has beliefs about various things in their lives and what goes on around them. They are obvious in the way people express themselves. Prejudicial statements such as, 'That political party is up to no good', or 'I don't like any of the people who listen to loud rock music', or , 'That religion is wrong', are clear and simple examples.

In dowsing, the proper dowsing state (q.v.) seeks an objective, distanced view of the world where the answer is welcomed, no matter how or in what way it might clash with pre-existing beliefs. However, many dowsers (and just as many non-dowsers) are unwilling to put their beliefs to one side for a while, or are even less willing to consider changing their beliefs in the face of evidence to the contrary.

This often means that such dowsers will use dowsing to bolster their pre-existing prejudices and biases when dowsing in areas about which they have strong beliefs. They are using dowsing to justify what they already believe in. And, because it is dowsing, because it is not open to reasoned argument, they can loftily declare that their dowsing upheld what they already secretly knew and accepted. For, after all, who can argue against them?

This, obviously, is not what dowsing is about. And, as such, it is probably wise to be circumspect about any dowser who holds very strong views about anything they say if they use dowsing to corroborate or justify their utterances.

A dowser who is concerned with being a good dowser (see GOOD DOWSER) is also one who is willing to face up to new views, new ideas, new concepts and be willing to at least consider them on merit. Any dowser who dismisses a new paradigm is using dowsing to bolster previously held beliefs. And that, sadly, is the mark of a limited and judgmental dowser. (See also PAST LIVES)

Beliefs also have an effect on the way the dowser interprets what is being dowsed. Thus, if there is a belief that all living things are radiating energies at specific frequencies, and that such frequencies can be detected using specific shapes, then a world view or paradigm will be developed which supports that view and adds further detail (and, hopefully, credibility) to it. In some cases, such beliefs will attract more dowsers who resonate with such an approach (See, e.g., RADIESTHESIA). Others will attract fewer proponents (See, e.g, LONG PENDULUM, THE).

Nevertheless, it is probably true to say that most dowsers will have a world view based on their beliefs, ruled by their dowsing discoveries, which they use to explain how the world works for them.

It is important for the novice or beginning dowser not to devote themselves completely to one or more of such paradigms straight away, but to gain enough experience so that they may be able to accept or reject such beliefs (or world views) because they will then have a greater appreciation of how they themselves see the world. They may well find that their beliefs have changed since taking up dowsing, to take in a more comprehensive view of possible explanations about the world around them. Those new beliefs, in turn, will naturally seek out other, supporting beliefs as nobody really likes being in a party of one!

It is an entirely understandable set of occurrences, but the dowser should always be aware that whatever paradigm is finally embraced, it is still a set of beliefs about how the world works. And, if the beliefs are strong, then the dowsing will naturally emphasize and reinforce that paradigm.

The more difficult, and more advanced position to adopt, is to have the mindset whereby any beliefs may be dropped at any moment in the face of what appears to be conflicting evidence. Such a paradigm is hard to maintain, but it does allow for fresher insights to occur and change to occur within the dowser.

Of course, if that latter sentence is not what the dowser intends in dowsing, then there will be less likelihood that the original beliefs will change. The dowser will, instead, become ossified in their view of the world, their beliefs will never change and they, in turn, will make no new discoveries. And that will deny them one of the greatest pleasures available to the dowser.

(See also THOUGHTFORMS)

∾

BIBLICAL REFERENCES

Dowsing, despite the wishes of many dowsers, is not directly and unequivocally referenced in the Bible. There are some very few verses which speak of the use of a rod (Exodus 17:4, for example), but, as a rod was also a symbol of authority, it is not clear that any such references are speaking directly about the same practice of dowsing as it is known today. It is entirely possible that some other cultural aspect was being referenced.

The problem with any such Biblical references is that they are highly unlikely to persuade anyone skeptical of dowsing to alter their opinion. The fact that there is no consensus amongst religious leaders about dowsing also makes for any religious agreement as to Biblical references problematic. Let us not forget, either, that for most verses which seem to propose one course of action of uphold one idea, there are always an equal number at least which can be read in such a way as to condemn that same approach.

The question worth asking, of course, is why does dowsing require this confirmation of its antiquity and respectability? The obvious response is that, if it can be proved that dowsing was not only mentioned but accepted in the Bible, then there is an automatic cloak of respectability. What is not clear, of course, is how such respectability from that quarter will enhance the overall acceptance of dowsing by, say, the scientific community.

The seeking of acceptance from the religious and scientific quarters is just a reflection of the general sense of being an isolated group in society.

If dowsing is to find a regular place in society, to come in from the cold as it were, then it is likely that the best and most effective way of doing that is to focus on the practical applications of the skill and how those can successfully, effectively and continually impact everyday life. It will not achieve that by finding dubious references from the past.

Most of the Biblical references talk of 'divination', which is not really the same thing. Divination (q.v.), by various means, is most commonly associated with telling the future, which is not what dowsing is primarily concerned with. In such cases, it is easy to see why those who 'divined' were condemned by God in the Bible, especially if they were wrong! (See also RHABDOMANCY)

There are about 130 references to a rod or staff as a symbol of authority in the Old Testament alone. However, it is up to the individual to consider whether such references make sense and have any value at all.

~

Binary Nature Of Dowsing

Because dowsing answers are one of two possibles (yes/no, true/false), it can be considered a binary system. Such a system may appear to be limited at first, but, when considering that computers are built on exactly the same model, it soon becomes apparent that it has a very wide range of applications indeed.

Once the model is accepted, then it is just a matter of ensuring that the question is capable of being answered in one of only two ways. Hence the more precise the question (q.v.), the more precise and useful the answer. In some cases, the dowsing might not appear to be asking a binary question. For example, dowsing a list, or determining direction. However, in each instance there is the underlying assumption that one item (in the case of the list) is correct and meets all the requirements of the question or that only one direction (in the second example) is the correct one.

~

Biophysical Effect

This is the term given to dowsing by Russian investigators of the phenomenon. Subsequently, they refer to the use of dowsing as the biophysical method.

The name appears to have originated in 1968 in a conference held in Moscow under the title, "Seminar on the Problem of the Biophysical Effect."

Since then, the interest in dowsing has not diminished and there is a steady stream of research taking place. (A reasonably well-documented account of this is to be found at http://www.seri-worldwide.org/id87.html (accessed Oct 2015) with references to to various publications.)

~

Biotensor

This is a quasi-scientific name for a dowsing tool which is designed or used primarily to examine the human energy field. Hence you will find descriptions of biotensor rods or bobbers.

It originates from the combination of 'bio' (life) and 'tensor' (movement, usually of muscle). However, the last part, 'tensor,' a mathematical term, could also be applied to coordinates in space, which is theoretically what is done to identify the extent of the human energy field.

~

BISHOP'S RULE

(See DEPTH, Method #2)

~

BLÉTON

Barthélmy Bléton (born c.1745), is one of the most notable of all water dowsers mainly because of the immense amount of interest, both popular and scientific, that was generated by his activities. He is also of interest in that he exhibited noticeable physical effects (q.v.) when over water. In fact, the physical effects he suffered were discovered when he was seven years of age and he became faint upon sitting on a stone, which was later found to be directly over a spring.

He was born in the Dauphiné region of France, which had long been (and continued to be) one of the areas which contributed a very high number of dowsers (or sourciers, as they were termed). Throughout his life, Bléton exhibited physical symptoms when over water.

He was extensively examined by Dr Thouvenel, a French physician, beginning in 1780. He was joined by Monsieur Jadelot, the Professor of Medicine in Nancy. Many other high-ranking officials also attested to the ability of Bléton to not only find water but also to follow the underground routes it took.

Breton used a curved rod (or baguette as it was referred to in the literature) which rested atop his outstretched index fingers. When water was present, the rod would rotate between 30 to 80 times a minute.

Thouvenel was convinced that electricity (q.v.) was the cause of the reaction and spent many hours devising experiments which would help prove that fact.

For a very detailed examination of the tests to which Bléton was put over the years, please refer to the relevant pages in *The Credibility of Dowsing* (2015) where they are translated from the French.

Bléton was, like so many other dowsers, attacked and 'revealed' as a charlatan. This time, it was by a young and brilliant French scientist, Monsieur de Lalande. He showed how easy it was to make the rod rotate by a small trembling of the hands. Like so many scientists, proving how something was physically to be done, he did not address what caused the trembling in the first place. Therefore, because he could make the rod rotate, the whole process was considered a fake. Such is still the prevalent method of dismissing the dowsing response. (See SCIENCE AND DOWSING)

Thouvenel eventually retreated to Italy due to adverse opinion to his work and also because of the coming French Revolution. He took Bléton with him and the latter died there some time after.

Of note is the fact that the Bishop's Rule for finding depth (q.v.) originated with Bléton when being tested by the Bishop of Grenobles.

The importance of Bléton in the history of dowsing is how well-documented his dowsing was and the variety of ways in which he was tested. He is the first such individual to be so well-documented.

BLIND SPRING

Normally a term used in the UK, a blind spring is the name given to an underground source of water which rises up towards, but does not reach the surface, instead radiating away through a number of horizontal fissures of varying depths.

The comparable term in the US is a water dome (q.v.).

(See also UNDERGROUND WATER)

～

Blink Dowsing

Blink dowsing is a type of deviceless dowsing (q.v.). In this form of dowsing, it is the body response as noted in the eyelids which gives the dowser the answer. As is usual, there is not one definitive response and it is up to the individual dowser to discover what constitutes a 'yes' and what is a 'no.'

The method is quite simple, although it might take some practice to begin with until the dowser is comfortable with this approach.

The eyes are soft-focused and the dowsing question is asked, after having got into the dowsing state (q.v.). A 'yes' response might consist of one or more blinks, or, conversely, of no blink at all. The same is true for the 'no' response. That is why it is important that the dowser knows which is which by practicing until the response is both swift and consistent.

The advantages of this type of deviceless dowsing are the speed and the obscure nature of it, so that dowsing may take place anywhere, anytime without being noticed.

～

Bobber

A bobber is a simple tool. It gets its name from the fact that the tip moves in a bobbing or swirling motion. There are various types of bobbers, but they all operate on the same principle, that of having a tip (weighted or not) at the end of a length of flexible material, the whole being attached to a wooden handle. The material might be a length of copper wire with several turns in it, acting as a spring. Or, it might be that an inherently springy material, such as a length of speedometer cable, is used instead, again being attached to a handle.

The earliest form was simply that of a long branch held out in front of the dowser. In use, its operation is more easily imagined as though it were a pendulum which, instead of dangling down from the finger and thumb, is held outwards. The movements of the bobber may therefore resemble those of a pendulum. Side to side motion, circular or up and down movements are all possible. The precise action to indicate a 'yes' or 'no' response from the tool is, like the pendulum, up to the dowser to establish for him- or herself. (See PROGRAMMING)

The choice of whether to use this tool or not really depends on the personal preferences of the dowser, although it is less useful outdoors when walking around, as the movement of the tip can become confused by the action of walking.

A more complicated version of a bobber is an aurameter (q.v.)

~

Body Sway

This form of deviceless dowsing (q.v.) is commonly taught as the first method of using the body instead of the tool. This is because this method rarely fails to get a response and is easiest for the dowser to see or feel what a deviceless technique is like.

Standing easily, with feet a little apart, the question is asked and the response is shown in the body. Assuming that the dowser was in a dowsing state, and the question well-formed, the response will usually be a movement forward for 'yes' and backward for 'no'.

The movement can be made more apparent by the dowser closing his eyes, thus making his sense of balance sharper. The movement might be only very slight at first and might take a moment to occur. This is usually because of an inborn reluctance to allow the body to respond. But usually the responses come quicker and with greater vigor once the initial movement has been experienced.

$$\sim$$

Bovis Scale

This is a scale (q.v.) arrived at by a French radiesthesist (see RADIESTHESIA) named A. Bovis from Nice in southern France, probably somewhere in the 1920's to 1930's. The original scale was based on the Ångström (1 Å = 0.1 nanometers, or 10^{-10} meters).

On this scale, a measurement of 6,500 Bovis was considered to be neutral for humans. Lower figures were thought to have negative effects and higher figures to have beneficial effects. Measurements above 18,000 Bovis (the scale originally went up to 10,000) were supposed to refer to the ethereal aspects of the world (i.e. non-physical).

If this scale is considered with reference to the Ångström scale, then visible light lies within the range Å 3,800 to Å 7,800. The neutral aspect at 6,500 therefore is red light. However, it is doubtful whether modern creators of the scale are aware of the original correlation to the Ångström unit.

The modern scale now goes up to 50,000 in most cases (although, as this is often a personal interpretation, there is no one standard (See THEORY OF RATES)), and it is sometimes said that the 'neutral' level of 6,500 has increased to 8,500, although with no real reason being given. In some places the Bovis scale is thought to be infinite.

The method of measuring is very simple. The dowser, with a scale before him, which can be purchased or drawn up using a simple straight edge, dowses along the scale to discover the reading for that particular target.

The problem with this scale is that it is not clear exactly what is being measured. There are terms such as 'radiation', 'measurement' or 'energy' (q.v.), used but with no real explanation of what they are referring to. However, there are those who point to some research on the spin of atoms with regard to the Bovis scale, claiming that those materials dowsed to be above 6,500 show a left or counterclockwise spin. Those below that number, show a right or clockwise spin. DNA is reported to have a left-handed spin, whilst cancer cells, for example, have a right-handed spin.

To further muddy the waters on this subject, the Bovis scale has also been suggested as representing the energy with which bio-photons are emitted. (This is a large area of study which has no direct bearing on dowsing. However, for the sake of clarity, the following is the definition of bio-photon from Wikipedia: "A biophoton (from the Greek βίος meaning "life" and φῶς meaning "light") is a photon of non-thermal origin in the visible and ultraviolet spectrum emitted from a biological system").

In summary then, the Bovis scale is really of use to the individual dowser only if he or she has a very clear and precise understanding of what they are using it for. And that would only become clear (or clearer) after a period of use and measurement of applicable subjects so that some sort of baseline was established against which subsequent measurements could be judged. Therefore, it would be more appropriate if some time was given to experimentation before making definite pronouncements. Indeed, this proviso applies to the use of all such scales.

C

Chance As An Explanation Of Success

See SKEPTICISM

~

Channeling

For some people, dowsing is sometimes confused with channeling. Channeling is a method whereby the channeler is acting as an intermediary for another intelligence, consciousness or similar. Whilst there may be an element of questioning in the process to obtain specific information, the channeler is not responsible for and has no direction over the resulting information. The whole process takes place while the channeler's own consciousness is not directly involved or engaged.

This is in contrast to dowsing, where there is a specific question asked, then a brief period (the dowsing state (q.v.)) where the answer is acquired. At no time should the dowser withdraw his or her own consciousness completely, but rather be aware of the world but in a less than engaged fashion. Also, in dowsing, the question is specific and the answer is brief and binary (see BINARY NATURE OF DOWSING) whereas channeling is a non-binary procedure and the answer is often not brief.

Some dowsers will seek to connect with their guide or protector (according to their beliefs and preferences) and claim that, as a result, the answers they receive are a form of channeling. This claim rests on the assumption that the answers to the dowsing question (q.v.) are coming directly and only from such guides or protectors. As there is no proof of this claim, only a belief, it is not a tenable position.

If the dowser claims only to be obtaining the answers from such an entity, then the question becomes one of the difference between communication and channeling.

It is quite possible to use dowsing as a form of communication (q.v.) as long as it consists of a series of clear questions and binary responses. Channeling does not meet those criteria.

In summary, a dowser seeks to maintain a clear awareness of the world whilst dowsing, a channeler surrenders that awareness whilst channeling.

(See also PROTECTION)

∾

CHARTS

Charts are a popular adjunct to dowsing. Their appeal lies in the fact that a number of possible answers can easily and clearly be seen in one place and one or more appropriate answers can be dowsed.

Charts can take various forms with fan and circular layouts being the most common.

The usual method is to have a pendulum with a point act as the device. The question (q.v.) is asked and the answer is given by the pendulum (q.v.) moving to point at one of the possible selections.

Charts can be very detailed and contain a large number of possible answers. The only important thing to remember, if you are going to construct your own, is to ensure that one of the possible answers is 'Other', as it is more than likely that there will come a time when the answer to a question is not accounted for by any of the options available. That might be due to simply forgetting, or due to new understanding which, in turn, allows for new possibilities.

There are various books containing large numbers of charts readily available, most of them are to do with personal growth or self-healing, although they can be constructed for any purpose.

The simplest chart could consist of a piece of paper sectioned off into four areas, with a possible answer in each quadrant. The most complex consist of several different categories of answers arranged in various ways (e.g. semi-circular, circular) on one chart.

(See also SCALES)

~

CHUNKING DOWN

This is a term applied to a way of reducing a large amount of information very quickly, to end up with the one piece of data required of the dowsing question.

A typical example might be trying to find the most appropriate Australian Bush Flower Essence by using the pack of cards which shows them all. It is easier to handle than the book, but the pack still contains a large number of possible answers.

By using the 'chunking down' process, the appropriate card can be swiftly discovered.

First, have a clear question (q.v.) in your mind; the purpose for which you are dowsing. Then, divide the pack into two parts and check which part the card you are looking for is in which meets the requirements of the question. Take that group of cards and divide it in two and repeat the question. By dividing the pack successively, after about three or four such divisions, you will be left with a small group of about four or five cards and they can be dowsed very quickly to select the right one.

Exactly the same process of dividing and sub-dividing can be used in something like a dictionary, or a long list of supplements, a gift catalog, a holiday brochure or any list of possible choices where it would be too tedious to dowse over each item, one at a time.

~

Clairaudience

Clairaudience is the acquisition of knowledge through hearing sounds, words or phrase. See CLAIRSENTIENCE.

~

Clairsentience

Clairsentience is the acquisition of knowledge by feelings such as emotions or other sensations. See CLAIRAUDIENCE.

~

Clairvoyance

Clairvoyance is the ability to 'see' the answer to a question or to gain information about a situation by having an internal vision, which may be more or less detailed.

Some dowsers have this ability and will sometimes get greater depth or complexity in response to a question as a result.

It is not a pre-requisite for successful dowsing. However, the more experienced dowsers tend to be able to develop clairvoyance along with their dowsing. In these cases, which are quite common, it appears that the activity of dowsing, carried out over a period of time, can stimulate the intuitive faculties. Therefore, some dowsers will experience clairvoyance whilst others will develop clairsentience (q.v.) or clairaudience (q.v.).

However, it is necessary to state clearly that the growth of such intuitive faculties is in no way essential in order to be a good dowser. All that is needed is practice and experience.

◞

Clearing

It needs to be stated quite clearly and categorically that 'clearing' (of energies or anything else non-physical) has nothing to do with dowsing.

However, there is still great confusion about this amongst many dowsers. You may come across descriptions of people twirling their pendulum (q.v.) saying that they are clearing something. However, what is actually happening is that they are using their pendulums to answer the (unspoken) question (q.v.) phrased something like, "Let me know when this clearing is done."

The clearing itself is done by intention (q.v.). The pendulum acts as an indicator to show when it has been done. Two separate activities performed at the same time.

Sadly, the movement of the pendulum has been confused with the act of clearing. This is due to weak thinking and poor teaching.

The only way that the movement of the pendulum could be equated with clearing would be by a radical new definition of what dowsing might be.

That seems totally unnecessary. Intention is well-known and can stand by itself as an activity which everyone can do to one degree or another. Dowsing is another well-documented activity which needs no further definition. It is the search for answers to carefully phrased questions by non-rational means. To try and cram intention into it is a pointless and useless waste of effort and does absolutely nothing to help distinguish dowsing as an activity in its own right and which, when carried out appropriately, is a superb tool to help understand where intention needs to be directed. It cannot and never will take the place of intention. The two are distinct activities.

If dowsing is ever to be appreciated more widely, then it would be hugely beneficial if such useless trappings were forever driven to the sidelines and recognized for what they are; useful but separate activities which need have no connection at all with dowsing.

$$\sim$$

COMMUNICATION

Communication can be considered one of the applications of dowsing. In this case, it must be accepted that any such communication will consist of question and answer, and that the answer must be binary in nature (See BINARY NATURE OF DOWSING). To borrow a telecommunication definition, this type of communication through dowsing would be considered duplex, in that there are two parties engaged in the communication, but it is a half-duplex system in that each party has to wait to communicate, in much the same way as two people using walkie-talkies can only speak one at a time.

Communication in this instance would involve either non-physical or non-human entities or both. Therefore, a dowser might communicate with her animal companion through a series of yes/no questions about, for example, the diet or exercise regime, to improve the quality of life.

Communication might also occur (again, through a series of yes/no questions) with such beings as devas or other non-human entities. Communication might be the best way to discover underlying reasons for environmental or health issues, or simply to improve one's relationship with the world.

However it is carried out, communication through dowsing will consist of a simple questions, answerable as either yes or no, and subsequent questions will develop from them until a complete picture is attained.

This procedure does not, however, dismiss the idea that a seasoned and competent dowser, through practice and familiarity, will not be able to also acquire *additional* information from such an interchange through such means as clairvoyance (q.v.) or clairaudience (q.v.), which are themselves versions of intuition (q.v.).

∾

Cup Stones

A cup stone is a saucer-shaped depression in a rock. They usually seem to date back to prehistoric times. Although there are various theories as to their purpose, they are mentioned here because they are an example of shapes which appear to have dowseable energies radiating from them. (See RADIESTHESIA) Such lines of energy (q.v.) can be tracked over long distances if one has enough patience and can maintain focus for a long period of time.

D

Depth

Finding depth is an invaluable skill, especially with regard to water dowsing, although the same principles can be applied to any underground dowsing target.

The particular method you choose will depend on your own preferences, but any two should give you the same answer.

Method 1:

Having located the target, remain standing over it and begin dowsing to find the depth. The usual method is to ask a series of questions, which can be answered 'yes' or 'no' which will allow the actual depth to be discovered. So, for example, the questioning could progress as follows:

1. Is the depth (to the top of the found water, for example) more than 300 feet? No

2. Is the depth more than 200 feet? Yes (*It is between 200 and 300 feet in depth.*)

3. Is the depth more than 250 feet? No (*It is less than or equal to 250 feet.*)

4. Is the depth more than 225 feet? Yes (*225 is between 200 and 250*)

5. Is the depth more than 230 feet? Yes

6. Is the depth more than 240 feet? No (*It is more than 230 feet and less than 240 feet.*)

7. Is the depth more than 235 feet? No

8. Is the depth 231 feet? No

9. Is the depth 232 feet? Yes

As you can see, it is a simple matter of breaking the measurement down into easily asked questions. The previous question's response determines the next question.

Start by finding the depth beyond which it does NOT lie and then backtrack to find the bracket. In the above example, it was discovered to be less than 300 feet down, but more than 200 feet. That is then the bracket in which the target lies. All that is then required is to narrow that bracket down until the target is found. In the above example, having found it was more than 200 but less than 300 feet, the bracket is found to be somewhere between 200 and 250 feet. Then it is found to be between 225 and 250, then between 230 and 240 feet, then between 230 and 235 feet, until the actual depth is found.

This method can be altered slightly by simply counting in units of, say, ten feet, and increasing the number until a negative response is given. Then the same process is applied to the exact depth. So, counting down in tens to 240 feet would get a No response at 240 in the above example. Then counting from 230 to 232 would find the exact depth. It is important that the dowser be very clear about which response is required. A negative response indicates overshooting the depth. A positive response indicates undershooting until the precise depth is met. That is found when the response goes from negative to positive and back again, as the depth is checked: "232 feet? Yes. 233 feet? No. 232 feet? Yes. Is the depth 232 feet? Yes." (Of course, it might be that, when using a pendulum (q.v.), a neutral swing (q.v.) is maintained until the depth is passed, at which point, according to the dowser's wishes, it might register as a Yes or a No. The point being that a change in motion is all that is required to bring attention to the first bracket to work back from.)

Method 2:

This is also referred to as the Bishop's Rule or Method, as it was first discovered, apparently, by the Bishop of Grenobles who took a close personal interest in the abilities of Bléton (q.v.) to find water underground.

Again, as in Method 1, the measurement begins from above the target. In this case, however, instead of counting to find the depth, it is measured on the surface. This is achieved by marking the location of the target, re-setting the dowsing tool and walking at right angles away from the target location. This is done until the tool indicates another reaction. This place is then marked and the distance between the two locations is the depth to the target.

When using this simple device, it is, of course, important that the dowser keeps in mind very clearly that he or she is looking for the secondary reaction to the initial target, not just any reaction at all.

Variation:

According to Charles Latimer, writing in 1876 ("An essay read before the Civil Engineers' Club of the Northwest, at Chicago, Feb. 1, 1875"), the distance can be computed in the following fashion. Assume that the dowsing tool begins to move at a certain point on the surface. Mark that point as 'A'. Where the tool completes its movement, which will be at the edge of the water, mark that as 'B'. The distance between 'A' and 'B' will be the same as from 'B' to the water source. This is the only mention of this method so far discovered and there may be issues with it being reliable, as the assumption is that the first movement ('A') relies upon the supposition that it is made to move at an angle of ninety degrees from the edge of the water. If that is the case (and it is not proven), then the nature of the intervening rocks could well alter the site of that reaction.

∾

DEVICELESS DOWSING

This is the term used for dowsing without any of the usual tools. Instead of having a response from a held instrument such as a pendulum or rods, the response is given by specific body reactions (or non-reactions) to the dowsing question (q.v.). The dowser usually waits to see what the response will be from a particular area of the body. For example, a sensation of heat or coolness in one area, or a tingling or a twitching, an ease of movement or a stickiness, movement in one direction or another: all these and more are variations of body responses to dowsing questions. It is up to the dowser to decide which area of the body; hands, fingers, eyelids, whole body, back of the neck and so on, is the area to be regarded as giving the response.

The interesting consideration from such types of dowsing is that the reactions, springing as they do from natural body movements and responses, would suggest that dowsing is an entirely natural skill, inherent in everyone. All that is required is that the body is listened to.

(See BLINK DOWSING, BODY SWAY and FINGER DOWSING.)

~

DIVINATION

Divination, or foretelling the future, is often associated with dowsing. This is because divination is usually (but not always) the result of wanting to know a specific outcome: in other words, the answer to a question. And that is what dowsing is about.

However, some people, because of that association, consider dowsing to be nothing more than divination. That is not so.

Certainly it is possible to ask questions about the future and to use dowsing to get answers. It is also true that some people seem to have a greater accuracy in that area than others. However, many dowsers do not do well in this type of dowsing. Although there is no definite reason why this might be the case, it is possible that the general uncertainty inherent in the future is not suited to a linear approach such as dowsing. A more simple intuitive approach may have better results and that might be due to the nature of intuition jumping any uncertainties and arriving directly at the future, rather than, as dowsing does, trying to get there incrementally with very restrictive questions which block out a more holistic interpretation.

Hence, for many people, divination will remain as a psychic ability. However, as previously stated, associating dowsing with divination is to think of it as a psychic ability. (This is also not the case, as is made clear in the entry on Psychics and Dowsing (q.v.)).

Divination is also carried out through the use of various instruments. A quick search for methods of divination will return a long list, usually around 100 items or more. The word itself comes from the Latin 'diviner,' to foresee or be inspired by a god. Merriam-Webster defines divination as, 'the art or practice that seeks to foresee or foretell future events or discover hidden knowledge usually by the interpretation of omens or by the aid of supernatural powers.'

Therefore, it is relatively easy to see that when a dowser, in the early days of finding minerals underground, has a movement of the rod, there being no obvious reason why it moves, it would be simple to say that supernatural powers were responsible, hence the act of dowsing was considered to be an act of divination.

Finally, rods used to foretell (See RHABDOMANCY) were usually referred to as 'virgula divina' (see DIVINING ROD) and confusion then arose between those rods and dowsing rods.

~

DIVINING ROD

This is a term applied, most usually, to the rod or other tool which was used to find water. However, it is not the most appropriate or correct term to use.

The term comes from the translation of the Latin phrase 'virgula divina' or divining rod. This is mentioned by writers in antiquity but it was meant to refer to rhabdomancy (q.v.) or divination by using rods or sticks. The efficiency, or effectiveness, of the divining rods relied upon the ceremony and the words or chants used in the process. In other words, the original use of the phrase was for something else entirely.

The Latin phrase for a forked or y-rod (q.v.), such as is associated with water dowsing (q.v.), is 'virgula furcata,' but that has not been taken up and is pretty much defunct as a term used in dowsing. It is asserted by some that this type of rod has its origins in the same era as the printing press. However, that is not much more than a supposition and can only be based on the use of it as described in Agricola's (q.v.) *De Re Metallica*. It is more than likely that such a rod was in use for some time prior to that, but exactly how far back is difficult to say.

Presumably, the use of the dowsing rod was associated with magic in the eyes of onlookers and it was thus an easy step to take to refer to the tool in the same way that Roman writers did; as an object for divining. (See DIVINATION)

~

Doodlebug

A doodlebug is the name given to any device which is used by a dowser to locate underground targets such as water, oil, minerals etc.. (See DOODLEBUGGING)

It appears that the name derives from 'doodle' which perhaps comes from a German word meaning fool or simpleton. Another aspect of the word is to waste time.

However, the other uses of the word; for a self-propelled railroad car, a jet-propelled robot bomb (both in the 1940's), and the larva of the tiger beetle (which is the original meaning, dating back to 1866), make this word one which appears to be gathered in to the language because something about it just sounded right for the activity being described.

~

DOODLEBUGGING

This is the name given to the activity of dowsing for underground targets such as water, minerals, oil etc. Its first use as applied to dowsing was in and around 1924.

~

Dowsing Applications

One of the questions which people inevitably ask about dowsing, when they first hear of it is, 'Apart from finding water, what else can you do with dowsing?'

This question is often answered by saying that you can ask any question about anything, or you can find lost objects. Usually, after this, the conversation takes a lighter tone and people talk about wishing they could find their keys or hundred dollar bills, before the topic is changed.

But the initial question is a valid one and deserves a decent response, because it is actually asking about all the ways that dowsing can be applied in your life. And it is worth taking the time to examine that aspect a little more closely.

The various applications of dowsing can be sub-divided into different categories to make the discussion easier to follow.

Firstly, there is the application of dowsing to real-world, physical targets, which are easily verifiable and often, but not aways, close at hand, if not always immediately visible. Of all the ways in which dowsing can be used, it is in this category that the most practical and personally useful dowsing takes place.

Obviously, the most commonly associated type of dowsing, dowsing for water, is in this category. Dowsing for water is an application where the target is either found or not, and, if found, is at the specified depth and flow rate or not. In other words, it is essentially a very practicable application, and like all such applications, the results are measurable and easy to verify.

Also in this category can be placed other practical applications such as finding lost objects, of which keys, rings, passports and so on are good examples of things we lose and really want to find.

Finally, the same principle, that of 'finding' and verifying, can be applied to locating plumbing, sewer and septic lines, wall studs, electric cables and other buried utilities.

If we now extend the target to be a physical one, but not close at hand or not immediately personally verifiable, then we can speak of dowsing being used in locating lost pets and people. It can also be used to fix a location, as in 'where did I park my car?', or 'Is the castle this way?'.

Extending the verification out in time instead of space, dowsing can be applied to such things as the best place (and/or time) for planting, the results of which will be evident later in the year. This simple gardening example can be extended easily to cover such things as dealing with pests and parasites as well as feeding your pet.

Moving from the plant kingdom to the animal kingdom means a simple change in the question, but it will essentially be the same type of question. The health and care of the animal can be dowsed and the results will be seen later on. And, of course, the exact same principle of dowsing to find the best things for health and welfare can be applied to humans as well, and the results will be evident or not.

Of course, such a small list of possible things to dowse about is only the tip of the iceberg in this category. As long as the target of the dowsing can be verified (is it where it was dowsed to be?, is the result as it was dowsed to be?), then it is fairly easy to consider many other ways in which dowsing can be used.

However, there is a second category of dowsing applications. This one consists of non-physical targets or results. It is not usually possible to verify anything, so it can also be called dowsing for information, not results. (However, this is not be confused with the misnomer of informational dowsing (q.v.), as all dowsing is ultimately to gain information.)

Those who engage in this type of dowsing usually do so in order to extend or deepen their world-view, their understanding of how the world works for them. So, someone who is having bad luck or a run of low-level illness might consider themselves to be the victims of a curse and would use their dowsing to discover the origin of such a thing, and how many curses they are suffering from.

Similarly, someone who is feeling not as secure as they would like, could dowse to find out if they had any angelic connections or protections. Another example of this type of dowsing would be to use it to ask questions of another being, not of this world.

In other words, this type of dowsing is generally used for self-interest and it is not possible to verify or cross-check any of the answers gained. They are purely and always personal (assuming, of course, that we are not referring to the professional use of dowsing for clients).

As a side note, however, such dowsing does not seem to stop some people from proclaiming that they have found the 'truth' of a particular scenario using such dowsing. They cannot be argued against for there is nothing to check. It is their version of reality which they are dowsing. But they often would like to impose that version on others.

So, in summary, the two main types of dowsing are 1) for verifiable results across a huge spectrum of topics from health to shopping to gardening and beyond, and 2) for non-verifiable research into an equally wide, potentially much wider, area of non-physical causes and effects as perceived by the dowser. It can thus be seen that there is something for everyone in dowsing. The innately practical and pure entertainment are both possible.

To become a good and competent dowser, however, it is important that practical dowsing is engaged in more frequently than the intangible type. As the more often you can verify your results, the better you will become by adjusting your questions or your protocol or both.

～

Dowsing Faculty

The dowsing faculty, that is, the ability to dowse, with or without a tool and obtain a definite and consistent response, is something which is very likely inherent in most people. Intuition (q.v.) is something everyone knows about and which nearly everyone has had experience of in one form or another. Dowsing can be considered as a form of focused intuition.

However, there is a difference between having such a faculty and exercising it. Some people will probably never use it for one reason or another; ignorance, skepticism and beliefs being the most obvious. Others might only use it occasionally or with mixed results and take it no further.

It is reasonable to ask, then, what proportion of the population (given that it is accessible and available to virtually everyone), might express this faculty in one or more areas of their lives?

The answer is probably somewhere within the region of twenty percent, but might be as low as five per cent, although one estimate in the 19th Century was for eighty percent. Some might only use it on rare occasions to find water. Others might use it regularly to assess diets and supplements. In most cases, people come to dowsing and to the use of it not much earlier than their thirties. Some few take it up earlier than that and many take it up much later. Go to any conference and you will find that those aged 40 and upwards are heavily represented with a few outliers of younger age.

The question which should be asked is why this is the case? It is reasonable to suppose that the younger age groups are more interested in other things, in making their way in the world, in finding out what they think and how they act. As middle age approaches, there is often a tendency to enter into a period of self-examination. At such times, dowsing seems to offer new insights as well as encouraging new skills.

Of course, everyone can dowse from a very young age. It is only when time, interests and beliefs change that the faculty is then expressed.

As an aside, it is worth pointing out that when young children, usually no older than 10 years of age, are taught to dowse, they all seem to take to it in a much more natural and easy-going way than adults do. They seem to accept, straight away, that it is something they can easily do and do well.

Whether this is due to a lack of inhibitions from which adults suffer, or to a clearer and less cluttered expression of the skill is hard to say.

~

Dowsing For Health

(See HEALTH DOWSING)

~

Dowsing State

The dowsing state is the state of mind a dowser should strive to be in after asking the question and before obtaining the answer. It is the state in which the dowser is best able to perceive the answer without skewing it through unwanted emotional bias.

Explaining what this state is and how to achieve are not quite such simple tasks, however.

To begin with, as everyone probably knows by now, the brain has various electrical impulses firing across it and that those impulses or brainwaves are associated with certain states of mind. So, for example, the normal, waking state is usually associated with what are termed Beta waves which exist between 13 and 30HZ (cycles per second). When you are asleep and dreaming, your brainwaves are usually in what is called the Theta band of between 4 and 7Hz. Very deep sleep is typified by the Delta state of anything from 0 to 4Hz. The Alpha state, by the way, is a restful waking state, but not as engaged with the outer world as the Beta state, and is between 8 and 13Hz.

The average person is experiencing one state or another, not multiple states at the same time. Meditative states reveal activity in the Alpha and Theta bands, with occasional Beta waves showing up. However, in an experiment which measured both sides of the brain, experienced dowsers exhibited an unusual spectrum of brainwaves in which all of the bands were active at the same time; Beta, Theta, Alpha and Delta. (The experiment was reported in the 'Sedona Journal of Emergence', October 2000, pp. 71-78, by Ed Stillman who carried out a neuropsychological study for the American Society of Dowsers. An earlier experiment with similar results was carried out in 1983. See *The American Dowser*, Vol 23, No. 1, Feb 1983).

Therefore, it would seem reasonable to suggest that, amongst experienced dowsers certainly, there is something going on in the brain which is unusual. It is this unusual state of mind which is the dowsing state.

Experience and repetition allow dowsers to enter this state very quickly. The way it is usually described is as a remote or detached frame of mind, almost like a slight withdrawal from the world whilst, at the same time, being able to hold a clear focus on the target or the question. The eyes tend to become soft-focused and the other senses are subdued as well, at the same time as focusing clearly and, whether using a tool or not, on allowing the body response to be clearly expressed by suppressing any emotional attachment to a particular outcome. This is why, when watching a dowser demonstrate, there is a moment of silence as they actually dowse. If a dowser is talking all the way through, then there is no possibility of a dowsing state being reached and the time is being used to illustrate a particular point, such as the optimal movement of a tool.

(See also MIND,THE)

$\sim$

Dowsing Tools

It is not the intention here to list all the possible dowsing tools which are either commercially available or can be made with relative ease by the dowser. Instead, it can be pointed out that virtually all tools used in dowsing are able to move because either they are held under tension or they are held in such a way that the dowser's tensed arms transmit their movements to the tool.

Examples of the first type would be the y-rod (q.v.), which is held under tension and can make swift and large movements in response to minor movements of the dowser's hands.

Examples of the second type would be the popular pendulum (q.v.) or l-rods (q.v.) which are allowed to move freely but respond, again, to the dowser's movements.

Thus a postcard, held in a flexed position, would be in the first category, along with watch springs, which were popular at the turn of the last century. A wedding ring on a thread and a bobber are example of the second category.

A dowsing instrument will fall into one of these two categories.

(See also BOBBER, AURAMETER, AUTOSCOPE, LECHER ANTENNA)

∾

Dualism

Although not strictly a dowsing topic, this concept of dualism can have an influence on dowsers and their interpretations of their results, and even of their questions.

By dualism is meant the dividing of the world, seen and unseen, into two and only two categories. Thus we hear of good and evil, of light and dark, of true and false, and of right and wrong. These are the most common ones.

By assuming that such definite categories exist, the dowser is automatically blocking out any other possibilities. Philosophically, of course, it is difficult to uphold any view that states an aspect of life is either one thing or another, and has no possibility of anything else.

This division can become a problem for those dowsers who uses their skill for such purposes as space clearing (q.v.). Here, carrying such a divisive view of the world into the practice of clearing (q.v.) will, almost naturally, set the dowser up as someone who is doing good and getting rid of something which is not good.

It is a sad truth that many dowsers have become very ill (and died) because they have seen themselves as being always in battle for the 'good' side against the 'evil' side. Their beliefs (q.v.) have acted upon them in such a way as to bring about what they feared. This is not the place to delve into the metaphysical viewpoints and arguments which such a view entails, but it is important to emphasize that it is less than helpful to have such a view of the world.

Just one argument will have to suffice. It is not possible that we, any of us, actually know and understand the complexity of the world, in energetic terms, in which we live. Therefore, the best judgment we can make at any time is whether or not what is found is serving the place or person involved and leave it at that, for what might be adverse to us humans might be of tremendous value to some animals or plants.

Blanket judgments obliterate such niceties and should be avoided wherever possible.

E

Earth Energy

Earth energy is a catch-all term for dowsing reactions which are not necessarily associated with water-dowsing or specific targets, but which are often presumed to be related to some aspect of the earth in general.

Thus, some of the confusing terms to do with ley lines (q.v.) are thought of as being earth energies. Similarly, some of the dowsed reactions around standing stones (q.v.), stone circles (q.v.) and other ancient edifices also come under this term.

It is an area of seemingly limitless research for those so inclined. One of the earliest investigators was Guy Underwood (q.v.), who set off lines of inquiry in the 1940's and 1950's which are still being investigated today.

In most cases, the investigation consists of finding plausible explanations as to why a dowsing reaction is taking place at certain spots, or attempting to correlate observed phenomena with energetic causes.

(See ENERGY and THOUGHTFORMS)

ELECTRICITY

During the late 19th Century onwards, the most common explanation as to how the dowsing tool might be moved was to assume that electricity was responsible.

This was especially true amongst the practitioners (principally water dowsers), who were in need of a simple explanation of what they were doing to their clients, and also, of course, to put their own minds at ease.

Because electricity was a recent discovery, and one which was having far-reaching influences culturally, it was natural that it was seized upon as being the most likely reason for the dowsing process. It had the advantage of being novel and exciting and relatively difficult to prove without an experimental setup.

The present theories about dowsing follow the same pattern, in that they also use the most recent and interesting discoveries in quantum physics and metaphysical thought to explain dowsing, which are also exceedingly difficult to either prove or disprove. (See HOLOGRAPHIC UNIVERSE, QUANTUM THEORY)

Therefore, the blanket explanation of electricity is definitely one related to the period of the late 19th and early 20th centuries.

However, it is important to point out that there is an element of truth in it, in that the flow of water underground through rocks does create a definite and measurable wave of an electrical nature and that there might be something in the theory, for specific dowsing applications.

However, as an over-arching explanation for the dowsing response in individuals in all cases, it seems unlikely, especially when considering distance dowsing, such as map dowsing (q.v.).

ELECTRO-MAGNETIC FIELDS

Over the years, there have been a variety of explanations to explain the dowsing response. Electricity (q.v.) was a very popular explanation from the mid-nineteenth century onwards. As a refinement of that, the idea that electro-magnetic fields could be responsible was mooted in the twentieth century.

One of the noted effects of water moving underground that there is a measurable field rising up in a narrow band above water, effectively delineating the sides of the water as it moves against the surrounding rock.

It is thought that the interference by the dowser of such fields is responsible for the dowsing response. However, if that is the case, then two issues remain to be resolved.

First, what about the dowser's physiology specifically is that can react to such fields? And, if that is discovered, then what is the range of such sensitivity which would bring about the response?

Secondly, this explanation, like all other such explanations, does not seem to take into account any other type of dowsing other than on-site dowsing (q.v.), such as finding water. Any dowsing to discover information not visible or accessible, or any form of map dowsing (q.v.), do not fit this theory.

This is perfectly OK, as long as physical interference with electrical fields, if proven, is not then touted as the one and only explanation for all applications of dowsing.

∾

Energy

Energy is one of the most overused terms in dowsing. It is used to describe any non-physical sensation or an invisible and supposed influence upon the subject at hand and, as such, has very little meaning beyond the fact that the dowser sensed or dowsed that something was (probably) there.

So, the term can be applied:

• to the state of a person's vitality,

• to a non-specific dowsed response over an object or person (presumably associated with a non-human aspect),

• as an explanation of the dowsing response itself, or

• as a subtle sensation the dowser has in a certain area or to a certain situation.

In other words, this is a term which, when used, is understandable only in relation to the circumstance of the sentence in which it appears.

By now, it is too firmly embedded in the dowser's general vocabulary to hope that it might be made applicable to only one area of dowsing. As such, be aware that it means many different things to each person and that the full import of what someone is trying to share is only going to be hindered by using this term.

If you use it yourself, then it would help listeners or readers to understand what is meant far better if there is some attempt to define or classify what is encompassed by the use of the word in the context of the dowsing target.

∽

Entities

Although they cannot be proven to anyone's complete satisfaction, there is a widespread belief, especially amongst certain sections of the dowsing community, that entities are real. By 'entities' is meant a conscious but non-physical being. Such things are supposed to interact with a person or a place in a way which is identifiable through the use of dowsing.

So, for example, suppose a place is considered by its inhabitants to be uncomfortable and uneasy to be in, then, one of the possible reasons for that would be the existence of entities there. Dowsing would be used to identify them and any number of possible methods could be applied to move them.

Thus, 'entities' can also serve to refer to what others would call ghosts.

The depth into which any dowser would go for describing them, detailing them and their types and various forms of influence would be very much a personal thing and need not necessarily be accepted by a fellow dowser as being the complete truth.

Entities then are very much up to the individual to identify and deal with. If the belief does not exist that they are real and have an influence on the physical world, then it is unlikely that a dowser would apprehend them.

~

Estimating Depth

See DEPTH

~

Ethics

The 'problem' of ethics was first brought to public attention due to the celebrity of Aymar (q.v.). How he used his skill in criminal and religious areas troubled the civil and religious authorities of the time.

Since then, ethics has only rarely raised its head sufficiently to be noticed by dowsers. It is true to say that the ethics of dowsing are rarely discussed in much detail in most classes today. However, this subject is perhaps one of the single most important areas to be aware of at all times.

The reasons for saying this is because of the very nature of dowsing itself. It is theoretically possible to ask a dowsing question about any conceivable subject. However, to be ethical, there are some questions which should not be asked. And this is not solely about the dowsing about the morality of others (as Aymar and other dowsers of that period had done).

To live ethically, to make ethical decisions, is not always clear cut or even easy to do. In essence, living ethically - as far as is possible - means to act respectfully to others and to understand your own reasons for those actions. In other words, it is not about intuition or gut feeling. It is, instead, about the 'right thing' to do. But knowing the right thing to do is not a hard and fast rule.

There are certain aspects of living which we, culturally, have accepted. Outright lying, murder, torture and so on are viewed the same across many cultures. They are the 'wrong thing' to do. But that leaves a huge range of possible actions open to debate. And that is where ethics comes into play; the consideration of what action to take in which circumstance.

Before examining the role of ethics in dowsing, it would be useful to take a step back and consider another relationship between the two. One of the benefits of dowsing, if dowsing is carried out carefully, with intelligence and forethought, is that a wider view of reality, of the world as it really is, develops. One of the natural offshoots of that, in turn, is that many dowsers will make conscious changes in their lives with the avowed aim of living a better life.

Now, the concept of a 'better' life is inherent in the idea of living ethically. Therefore, it should be the case that, as dowsing experience and knowledge grow, so the dowser's relationship with the world around him or her changes and thus it becomes easier to make ethical choices because of that awareness.

But, for the novice dowser, or the dowser who has not had the benefit of dowsing in areas which will allow a new perspective to develop, the ethics of dowsing might not seem obvious.

Having said that, however, there are some general rules which, if followed, will allow a more ethical viewpoint to develop. Paramount amongst these rules would be never to dowse about another person without their express permission. Although nobody can really claim to know for certain how dowsing works, it seems highly likely that there is some type of energetic engagement with the object of inquiry. Therefore, to dowse about another person; their state of health, their morals, is to become entangled with them on some level. Or, to put it another way, it would be similar to going into their home without an invitation and poking into all of the closets, cupboards and drawers you want to. Hardly a 'polite' way of being and certainly not one which would imply that you are living a 'better' life!

Another way of looking at the whole question of ethics as it relates to dowsing is to take the time to consider whether you are dowsing about something because you can, or whether it is about something which is pertinent to you. If you are dowsing out of idle curiosity, or want to convince yourself that you are going to find something out for the greater good, then that is being unethical.

An example will help illustrate the problem.

Suppose you have a distant friend who you hear is unwell. You decide to dowse the problem and tell her what you found and give your suggestions as to how to improve her health.

That is unethical. You did not ask her directly. It was something you wanted to do, and because it felt like a friendly thing to do, you went ahead and did it. But, given the fact that you have no idea what the real issue was, whether or not any course of treatment was being followed, and, more importantly, whether or not she actually wanted you to dig around inside her energy field, then it was for purely personal satisfaction and actually had nothing to do with you. Your friend's health is her concern, not yours. Until she asks you to help.

Other examples could include dowsing about a person's habits, what they are doing, why they are doing it. None of those topics are of any concern except that person's.

Just because we can dowse about anything does not give us the automatic right to do so.

Perhaps it might be easier to end this discussion by emphasizing the positive aspects, rather than giving negative examples.

Ethical dowsers stick to what is pertinent only to themselves, unless specifically asked otherwise.

Ethical dowsers are generally more interested in understanding how they function in the world and try to deepen and broaden that understanding through their personal relationship with the world.

Ethical dowsers have clear personal boundaries, in their life and work. They also tend not to feel like victims and are willing to adopt new perspectives as they are discovered.

Ethical dowsers never display the results of their dowsing just for the acknowledgment and praise. In fact, they rarely reveal their answers anyway because such things are usually of no interest to anyone else but themselves. They might be more willing to share their questions and their reasons for those questions, however.

In summary, the whole business of ethics can appear to be a tangled mess. Yet it is surprisingly simple if you consider that it comes down to you wanting to be a better person. If you don't, no amount of examples, persuasion or debate will make you ethical. You are either ethical in your dowsing habits, or you are not. If you want to be a better person, then you will automatically apply more ethical consideration to what you do and what you dowse.

Being ethical is a process. It will involve giving up some habits and adopting new ones. The speed of this change and the amount of change is up to you, but the end result is being a person you can feel more and more proud of.

Note: At the time of writing, the British Society of Dowsers has a code of ethics (https://www.britishdowsers.org/code-of-ethics/) which is worth reading. There is also a code there for professional dowsers (those registered with the BSD). A search of the American Society of Dowsers website (http://dowsers.org) does not reveal any mention of ethics, nor does there appear to be any mention of ethics on the Canadian Society of Dowsers website (http://canadiandowsers.org)

(See also PERMISSION)

F

Fallacies

There are several fallacies which have spread over time about dowsing. Their existence is due mainly to poor or no teaching of dowsing as well as the unwillingness to think critically. Their continued existence weakens the real strength inherent in dowsing by acting to confuse and obfuscate the central truths of this skill.

What follows is a collection of the most well-known fallacious ideas held, both by dowsers and non-dowsers.

First is the idea that dowsing is a special skill or gift available to only a chosen few and that you have to be born with the gift. Absolutely not! The proof of this is that pretty much any child will happily and easily begin to dowse with very little help, once shown the general principles. Further, any adult is able to dowse, given sufficient time as well as being able to find a method works best for them. Not everyone is able to dowse equally well and some will prove stronger than others in certain specific areas. But the fact remains, dowsing is an innate human skill, accessible by all and limited only by their beliefs (q.v.) and by opportunity.

The second of these fallacies (in no particular order) is that the tool does all the work. Dowsers are often overheard saying such things as "My pendulum cleared the energies", or, "My pendulum told me that…".

Some, perhaps, say this without thinking, but others do use it meaningfully. Some dowsers do actually believe that the pendulum, by some sort of motion, actually does do some sort of work. Maybe it does, but that work is not part of dowsing. Put as simply as possible, a pendulum (q.v.) or any other tool, by itself, left alone will do nothing at all. It requires the focus and intention (a separate mental state from dowsing! - See below) of the dowser to achieve anything.

Another fallacy is that something else moves the tool. The point to bear in mind is that as you are the one holding the top, you are the one making it move. Although it might be argued that the reason for moving the tool (see IDEOMOTOR EFFECT) might lie outside of your conscious awareness, nevertheless the tool is moved by the dowser.

A fourth fallacy is that dowsing and intention are the same, and that by merely swinging a pendulum, with the intention to do something like clearing or healing, dowsing is taking place. This is eminently wrong. It is dealt with under Intention (q.v.)

A fifth, and most pernicious, fallacy claims that dowsing is a healing method. This fallacy is dealt with more extensively under Healing (q.v.).

Another one claims that a tool should not be handled by another person for fear of some form of energetic contamination.

Still another claims that specific dowsing jobs or targets require specific tools, such as crystal pendulum for certain tasks and a metal one for others. The point here is that they are all just tools and if you believe that a certain thing is true, then it will be for you. This is also true for the previous fallacy. (As Henry Ford once said, "If you think you can, or think you cannot, you are right".)

As for confusing dowsers and psychics in general, see the relevant entry; Psychics and Dowsing.

Feng Shui

Feng Shui, the Chinese art of placement, is often held as being one of the earliest practices in which dowsing was used. The picture of Emperor Kuang Yu, founder of the Hia dynasty (2205-2197 BC), is often used to prove the ancient nature of the skill.

Feng Shui certainly does use dowsing, but it is not certain that the Emperor was also a Feng Shui practitioner.

To explore further the use of dowsing as it can be applied in Feng Shui is beyond the scope of this volume. Interested readers should first learn the basics of Feng Shui and then how dowsing can be applied to it.

~

FINGER DOWSING

Finger dowsing is a type of deviceless dowsing (q.v.).

There are several ways in which a dowser can use his or her fingers to get a dowsing response. What follows are the major methods of this technique. In all of the following examples, the basic premise remains the same, which is that the muscle response will be weaker or slower for a negative response than it will be for a positive or truthful response. This premise is the basis for all kinesiological testing, whether performed by a chiropractor or a dowser.

Method 1:

Take the middle finger and bend it over the top of the index finger. Pressure is then applied and the index finger will either bend easily or slowly and with resistance. In most cases, a weak response (bending quickly) is a negative and the opposite is positive.

Method 2:

Form a ring with the thumb and index finger of the non-dominant hand and then, using the index finger of the other hand, strike at the point where the other index and thumb meet. If the ring breaks (weak), that is usually negative.

Method 3:

As in method 2 above, first form a ring with the thumb and index finger of one hand. Then, create a link, as if in a chain, by putting the thumb and index finger of the other hand in such a way that each ring has the other ring inside. The dowsing response is found by trying to pull the rings apart. If the chain breaks (weak), that is negative.

Method 4:

Again, form a ring with the non-dominant index finger and thumb. This time, press the index and thumb of the other hand together in a tight pinch and press that into the ring formed by the other hand. The dowsing response is very much the same as before. The pinch inside the ring will either open easily (weak - negative) or remain closed.

Method 5:

Take the index finger of the dominant hand and find a smooth place where the ball of the finger can be rubbed back and forth easily. A table top is perfect for this. The weak response (negative) is when the finger slides easily across the surface. A strong response (positive) is when the finger movement feels 'sticky' and has some resistance.

Method 6:

A variation of Method 5, this where the balls of the thumb and index finger are rubbed against each other gently. Again, a weak response (negative) would be a smooth movement, where a positive response would be a feeling of 'stickiness' and a sensation that there is some resistance to the movement.

The interested dowser might well find further variations which work well for him or her.

~

FUNDAMENTAL BEAMS

These may also be referred to as fundamental rays. This is a term used (mainly in Europe) to describe the direction and length of dowseable beams (or rays) emanating from different materials. Thus, a sample of salt would produce beams of sodium and chloride. Placing other elements on these beams, dowsing will either show they have disappeared or become much stronger (longer). Such variations are supposed to show how the interaction of various chemicals either complement or negate each other.

This is an area where it is difficult to prove very much and that the dowser's own preconceptions are probably very much to the fore. (See RAYS OF UNION)

G

Geobiology

See BAUBIOLOGIE

~

Geopathic Stress

This is a term often used by dowsers who are drawn to space clearing (q.v.). It is relatively recent in origin. However, despite that (or maybe because of it), there is only a general consensus as to what it refers to.

Some will use it as a means of describing an environment ('The land suffered from geopathic stress due to underground water streams'), while others will use it as a means of describing a wide range of symptoms or conditions caused by those environmental issues ('He was suffering from geopathic stress'). One, therefore, is descriptive of an environment while the other is referring to effect of that environment.

Geopathic stress is included here because of the early connection between health and environment confirmed originally by Gustav von Pohl (q.v.) at

Vilsbiburg(q.v.), and later by the University of Vienna's 1989 study on the short-term consequences of humans in such locations. The report was called , "Research into the Biological Influences of Geopathic Locations."

Since that time geopathic stress has been something which dowsers have sought and identified. This is because they are, presumably, able to identify and react to areas of disturbance in the Earth's magnetic field. This disturbance is a commonly agreed upon cause of geopathic stress.

Again, as with so many other aspects in dowsing, there is a lack of uniformity in descriptions and classifications. The basic area of agreement is that conditions within or on the surface of the earth can and do cause a range of symptoms in humans, animals and plants which are, to a greater or lesser degree, measurable.

Causes of geopathic stress are considered to include underground streams, cavities, fault lines and mineral formations, as well as human constructions such as pipe lines, tunnels, graveyards and the like. Outside of these agreed areas there are others such as Black Streams (a Feng Shui (q.v.) term) and even ley lines (q.v.). Indicators of geopathic stress are considered to include the presence of energy grids (q.v.) and how they relate to each other as well as interact with underground (or overground) energetic disturbances. There is no common agreement on such things.

It is not the purpose of this present volume to go into details about how to detect geopathic stress, its symptoms or how to deal with it, as such areas would take us away from the central concern of dowsing. There is a range of such information readily available and the interested reader is encouraged to pursue such leads as interest him or her. Please always bear in mind that much of what is written is biased to present the author's viewpoint as being the sole true one. It is highly doubtful that any one person, no matter how well-informed, has a complete version of the truth of the reality of geopathic stress.

∾

GERMANY

The earliest documented dowsing comes from Germany where the skill was used to discover metallic ores for mining purposes. The activities associated with this industry are clearly illustrated in the work by Agricola, *De Re Metallica*. (See AGRICOLA)

It was from Germany that miners, using the skill of dowsing, came to England in the 16th century to help develop the mining industry of the south-west. It is interesting to note that the same area was still considered to be one of the most important centers for dowsing over 200 hundred years later.

~

GOOD DOWSER

First, it should be established what is meant by the term 'a good dowser'. To some people, it might mean being very accurate, as in 100% or very close to it.

However, a good dowser is not determined solely by accuracy (q.v.); and it should be recognized that no dowser is ever 100% accurate all the time.

There are, however, various factors which need to be taken into account.

First, a good dowser is someone who is able to dowse well by asking good, detailed questions (q.v.). Secondly, he or she should be ethical (see ETHICS) at all times, and thirdly, the results should be bear out the general accuracy to be far better than chance.

As an addition, most good dowsers are also interested in personal growth (q.v.) and use the skill to advantage for themselves.

Therefore, if those are the major attributes of being a good dowser, then it becomes obvious that it takes time, practice and effort applied consistently to be good.

It is common for beginner dowsers to have a high success rate which then tails off. But, as they have had little experience of various types of dowsing and have not had sufficient time to learn their own strengths and weaknesses, or to develop well-formed questions, they may well become good dowsers, but that is something which will only become obvious over time.

~

Grids

The grids referred to here are what are generally considered to be energetic grids arising from the Earth in some fashion. Detailed consideration of these grids is beyond the scope of this volume, as it would open up several areas which have no direct connection with dowsing. Such areas would include discussions of the origins and purpose of any such grids.

Given that proviso, there is still some areas of interest directly relating to dowsing and grids. Firstly, there are two supposed grids which have been discovered or revealed which have a marked effect (again, supposedly) on health. These two grids, respectively the Hartmann and Curry Grids, are frequently brought into discussion of space clearing (q.v.) because of the negative effects they have on health.

However, it is important to make note of some pertinent points here about both these grids in particular and Earth grids in general.

Firstly, all such grids are not equally accessible to all dowsers. Some dowsers find them with great ease, whilst others will struggle to locate them at all. This does not mean that they do not exist, but it might mean that such grids are more liable to be found by those people invested in finding them.

Secondly, overlaying the Hartmann and Curry Grids, for example, on the earth would mean that, towards the poles, there is virtually no room at all between grid lines as they all converge upon the poles and there would, presumably, be real health issues for all those living beyond the Arctic Circle. This is certainly not proven.

Thirdly, if one considers the nature of the grids, there is what appears to be a cultural bias. To explain this, it is necessary to consider the Eastern concept of earth energies against the Western concept. In the East, arising from the Feng Shui (q.v.) tradition there are very few, if any, straight lines in their perception of negative or positive earth energies. In the Western tradition, however, the entire basis of earth energy relies upon such straight lines being found. This is not only the case in ley lines (q.v.) which are also brought into the grid concept by some, but equally obviously in the Curry and Hartmann Grids. Could it be possible that such interpretations of the energies within the earth are themselves the result of the culture in which they were 'discovered'? Regularity and order tend to mark the Swiss and German cultures, whereas the same principles are not in evidence in the philosophy of ancient China where Feng Shui originated. A more fluid concept of harmony, of balance, was prevalent then. Perhaps this is what is reflected in the moving elements of Feng Shui such as Black Streams and Dragon Lines.

Whatever your particular view is concerning grid lines and their effect on humans, it is very important to remember that what you dowse as being present and 'true' may not necessarily be confirmed by a number of other dowsers, and vice versa.

This idea of grids around the earth is certainly an intriguing one but is not necessarily a complete picture by any means. There are those who suggest that a 'crystalline' grid, based on the idea of Platonic solids, is evident around the earth. (Yet that does not seem to take into account plate tectonics: the movement of the continents over time.) Whether there is any truth to this or not, whether such things can be dowsed independently or not, rely mainly upon the individual dowser's bias and beliefs.

As mentioned elsewhere (see BELIEFS) if a dowser is sufficiently convinced that a set of circumstances is correct or in existence, it is more likely than not that any subsequent dowsing will confirm such a belief. That is why it is so difficult to be truly objective in dowsing.

In summary, if you as a dowser believe in a grid system and that it has certain negative effects, it is highly likely that your dowsing will support that belief. But, it is equally important to consider that whatever the 'truth' of the situation is, it is highly unlikely that as inhabitants on the skin of a giant being we have been able to map out or understand the full energetic nature of the earth. It is more than likely that any such understanding we have now is going to be superseded by fresh and more detailed information as time goes by.

Therefore it is the opinion of this volume that any such understanding (or dowsing) of any grid system should be thought of, at best, as a work in progress and vastly limited in perception. (See also TRUTH)

H

Healing

Many people associate dowsing with healing. They are wrong.

While dowsing can be used to identify areas or issues which need healing, dowsing is not something which can be applied to bringing healing to them. Healing, in the sense of bringing areas into balance, is something which is done by intention. Some people have been wrongly taught, or shown, that twirling a pendulum (q.v.) whilst setting the intention (q.v.) to heal means the pendulum itself was in fact actually performing the healing.

The pendulum supposedly stopped when the healing had been done. What actually was going on was intention was being sent and the pendulum was merely showing when it had happened. But the action of intention and motion of the pendulum were then confused with each other and it was then believed that the pendulum was doing the healing, and, because the pendulum was used in dowsing, it was therefore dowsing which was doing the healing.

This, of course, is not the case, as the above explanation makes clear. However, some teachers have gone further and maintained that by twirling the pendulum one way, some sort of energy is being taken out or moved or changed in some fashion, and that twirling it in the opposite direction puts energy in or creates new energy in some fashion, as if the pendulum, in and of itself, has such ability!

It cannot be stated often enough or loudly enough that this is simply not true, but is the wishful thinking of those involved. Dowsing is, and always has been, the seeking of answers to questions which the rational mind cannot furnish.

To suddenly assume that a pendulum's movement can bring about healing and then to assert that that fiction is what dowsing is, is adding confusion to stupidity. One can only assume that such irrational ideas have been propagated either by those who wish to make a profit from presenting such 'knowledge' as a healing modality, or by those who are totally unaware of what they are actually doing and have no real conception of what dowsing actually is. If it is the former, then it is just another example of someone taking advantage of others' ignorance and gullibility to make money. And, if the latter is the case, then the blame for such ignorance must lie with those who teach and uphold such views, or who are uninterested in actually learning to dowse properly.

There is also a tendency to refer to something as pendulum healing (q.v.). In this case, there is an assumption being made that there is something about a particular pendulum, the properties of which allow it to be able to bring about healing in one way or another. In some cases, it is the supposed shape and in others, the composition of materials which brings this about. (See RADIESTHESIA) In either case, although there is nothing inherently wrong in referring to the process as 'pendulum healing', the fact that it is carried out using a pendulum in motion does cause confusion amongst some people (both new and experienced dowsers) that what they are witnessing is dowsing in some form, when that is certainly not the case.

The pendulum itself is not what is dowsing. It is the person holding it; the dowser. Substituting one for the other is unhelpful and, literally, thoughtless.

Dowsing is a method of accessing knowledge. Healing is therefore not dowsing. And the sooner that is accepted amongst the dowsing community, the quicker dowsing will be seen and accepted by a wider section of the world.

∾

Health Dowsing

Health dowsing is one of the most popular applications of this skill. However, there is a danger in using the term as it is too often confused with healing (q.v.). Although it is said elsewhere, it is worth repeating that dowsing is not healing.

What, then, is health dowsing? It is the application of dowsing to determine the most effective course to follow in order to reach certain specific health goals. Thus, health dowsing can be considered to encompass any or all of the following (given certain, specific goals):

◆Which vitamin and / or supplement regimen would be most effective

◆Which exercise program would be most productive and least problematic

◆Which foods would be best avoided

◆Which dietary regime would be most effective with fewest unwanted side effects

◆Which supplements / herbs / other would be most effective to deal with specific physical issues with the least side-effects

In other words, health dowsing is a method of evaluating and assessing possible solutions to specific issues facing the dowser. And, as such, it is very useful as it it is something which is measurable. That means that the dowser can see, by personal experience, the accuracy of his or her dowsing. This is valuable information and can, through understanding the process of goal setting and questioning, help the dowser to improve significantly.

∾

High Self

The 'High (or 'Higher') Self' is a concept which is reasonably common amongst various religions but is not very clearly defined. It is probably fairest to say that the High Self is generally considered to be some metaphysical aspect of each individual which is, in some way, connected with the universe, the Divine, God or whatever the perception is of the ultimate aspect behind creation.

In dowsing, some dowsers prefer to call upon their High Self either for protection (q.v.) or as a connection to the source of the answers they are seeking. Again, this is never really clearly expressed and is usually just considered to be a factual state of affairs once the prayer or whatever ritual has been followed.

This seems to have become more prevalent after the arrival of the New Age in the last quarter of the 20th Century and has been added on, in most cases, as a step preparatory to actually dowsing. As such, it is, of course, unnecessary.

One of the reasons for doing this is probably due to a dualistic view of the universe (see DUALISM). There is the element of protection (q.v.) inherent in this process, as it is assumed that the High Self has the body's best interests at heart. (Although there is no rational ground for assuming any such thing, as the physical body's best interests might not necessarily coincide with the view of the High Self. And 'best interests' usually has the implication of being something good, happy or generally 'nice' - not a tenable argument.)

Another reason is probably psychological in that, by linking in some fashion to another being, the dowser is distancing him or herself from the answers and thereby absolving themselves from liability if their dowsing proves to be wrong.

As an aside, this concept seems to be much more widespread in the U.S. than elsewhere.

~

HISTORY OF DOWSING

Most dowsers, from time to time, will wish to discover the historic lineage of their skill. They want to find out how far back it goes in time.

One of the reasons for this desire is to prove the antiquity of it, and therefore, by association, the validity of it. The idea being that anything which can be proven to be very old must be true and real. In other words, the history of dowsing is often sought as a way of facing down the arguments of skeptics. The history will act as comfort blanket. And the need for that blanket, of course, arises from the feeling that dowsing is misunderstood or under-appreciated and is isolated from the mainstream of society. And we all want to be accepted, don't we?

Another reason for unearthing the history of dowsing is to see how it has changed over time. What began as a search for minerals, became a search for water, and then it extended into the field of health and to the invisible. Today, dowsing encompasses a vast field of applications and uses. That diversity happened over time.

Perhaps the best current examination of dowsing history is that contained within Christopher Bird's book, *The Divining Hand*. Rather than attempt a potted version of that, it is easiest to refer to the book instead.

The recorded (written) history of dowsing is, by and large, fairly well covered and there is broad agreement about it and about the twists and turns it has taken over the past 400 years.

However, many dowsers wish to push the search back much further (for the reasons stated above), and there are many attempts to explain certain Biblical references (q.v.) as being about dowsing. Others push further back and refer to the possibility that Egyptians dowsed, or to Chinese Feng Shui references (q.v.). There are those who refer to cave drawings such as those at Tassili n'Ajjer in Algeria which, they claim, show dowsing being used.

Although, intellectually, it is interesting to speculate about such things, there is no definite proof in any of the above, only speculation tinged with hope.

However, if dowsing is considered as being a natural human skill which sometimes uses tools, there is no need to search for proof. Humans have always had this skill and exercised it in various ways at various times.

Therefore, to search for proof of this is like searching for proof that earlier humans breathed air. Of course they did, but there are no prehistoric records showing this. There is no need.

In much the same way, the history of dowsing is unwritten and unrecorded for the reason that it was a natural and everyday skill. And that skill was not named dowsing in earlier times.

∾

HOLOGRAPHIC UNIVERSE

The holographic universe is another explanation put forward to explain how dowsers acquire their answers when dowsing about subjects which are not tangible. The theory is certainly not complete nor its fundamentals accepted. However, in outline, it runs somewhat in the following manner.

It is possible that one explanation of how the universe works might be due to seeing it as composed more of information than the 'normal' two states of matter and energy, which, in this case, would be incidental to the information, or the primary state of the physical world. Through various aspects of physical theory, including string theory and the study of entropy, it is possible to assume that the universe we sense is, in fact, a hologram and that three-dimensional space does not really exist. That would mean that distance doesn't really exist. Which, in turn, means that nothing is truly separated from anything else. All is interconnected at some level.

If that theory of physics is eventually proven, and as yet there are some interesting theories but a lack of convincing evidence, then the assumption is that dowsers (and non-dowsers, of course), can, in some fashion, simply reach out and have the answer to any question of this universe immediately to hand.

While it is an engaging and attractive theory, it does, of course, have flaws in that, even if true, how is the information accessed? What part of the mind or brain (or other organ) is responsible and how is it possible to 'switch' it on or off (assuming that is what happens)?

Nevertheless, this theory is quite popular amongst dowsers. This might be due to the fact that quantum physics is involved to a degree and this has a powerful draw amongst many in the new age community as a means of explaining much that 'classical' science cannot embrace. And because quantum physics is incredibly difficult to explain, yet seems to offer so many strange insights, it has a great attraction as a glib and almost understandable source of all possible answers.

(See QUANTUM THEORY)

Hydration

Hydration is required for the body to function properly. Drinking water, not other liquids like coffee, soda, beer, etc., helps the cells to function at optimal efficiency. This is necessary given that the dowsing response, the movement of the tool or the body response in deviceless dowsing (q.v.), is purely physiological.

It is considered to be a good health practice to drink sufficient water every day, no matter whether you are dowsing or not. As each person's body response to water will be slightly different, you will need to discover what is the optimal water intake for you and to ensure that you have met that level prior to engaging in any dowsing, if you wish to dowse with greater accuracy. (See ACCURACY)

Hypersensitivity

Another possible explanation for some on-site dowsing (q.v.) results is the fact that some people have been shown to exhibit hypersensitivity in one or more of their physical senses. In particular, hypersensitive hearing has been posited as one of the means by which 'supposed' dowsers are able to locate underground water when no surface clues exist.

It is known that certain individuals have very sensitive hearing, able to clearly discern what are normally considered very low levels of sound. For example, one woman was able to hear telephone conversations by listening to the wires.

This fact, by itself, has, in the past, been used to suggest that water dowsers are such hypersensitive people and that they can detect the sound of water flowing through underground channels.

This was offered as a possible theory during the nineteenth century, but seems to have fallen out of favor now. However, it might still be a valid explanation in a certain limited number of cases!

∾

Human Body, The

It is natural that a good amount of research has been conducted on the human body to attempt to identify how the dowsing reaction takes place. Is there some gland or organ which is responsible, or is it a more diffuse aspect?

In order to answer these, the human brain has been evaluated (See DOWSING STATE and THEORIES) as have various parts of the body.

It is interesting to note that the results of various experiments made (both to test dowsing, as well as to investigate other areas), have shown that the human body is an incredibly sensitive construct able to react, at least on the unconscious level, to very, very small stimuli. For example, extremely low EMF's can affect the heart and pulmonary system, as can solar winds and cosmic rays. The immune system responds to light and your melatonin production is sensitive to blue light. (See SENSITIVITY)

In other words, the human body is known to be highly sensitive in a number of ways to a huge variety of stimuli. Therefore, theories of dowsing (q.v.) which seek to use one stimulus to explain what happens may well be restricting possible explanations by excluding so many others. Indeed, it might well prove that a synthesis of responsive systems within the body to a variety of stimuli is ultimately responsible for the dowsing phenomenon.

What can be gathered from such experiments is that there is no clear and well-defined physiological aspect which can be claimed to be responsible for the dowsing reaction. Whatever physiological claims there may be for identifying how water is detected underground would not seem to be acceptable claims for other types of dowsing, such as map dowsing (q.v.) or health dowsing (q.v.)

I

Ideomotor Effect

The phrase Ideomotor Effect, (originally termed the 'ideomotor action,' also called the Carpenter Effect), comes from 'idea' (idea) and 'motor' (muscular action). The phrase was coined by William Carpenter in 1852. He believed that it was possible that there could be muscular movement without any conscious desire or emotion.

In its simplest form, the term means that there is an unconscious idea or direction in the mind and the body then follows it, without there being conscious awareness of any such connection. The body has many unconscious responses as part of living; the narrowing of pupils in response to bright light, for example, or shivering when cold. This is your body responding to stimuli without your being conscious of the fact.

In much the same way, simple motor behavior can be affected by ideas or emotions in the mind when holding a dowsing tool.

It has been examined and proven in many cases over many years that this effect is behind much of the so-called spiritual or paranormal 'forces' supposedly acting on people.

The coining of the term correlates with the rise in interest in spiritualism in the 1840's, with its attendant activities such as the Ouija board (actually an early form, using a planchette—a wheeled writing board) and table turning. The popularity of such activities naturally attracted scientific investigations, one of the results of which was this term.

Because dowsers do not seem to have any conscious control over the tool when they dowse, this idea has been widely adopted as the reason behind the tool's movements.

The explanation is one which has been widely adopted by dowsers as being the reason for the movement of the tool but there is no agreement at all on what causes the unconscious idea which precedes such movement.

It is certainly true that accomplished dowsers are not aware that they are in any way directing the tool to move, but beyond that, the possible theories for initiating such movement are open to conjecture.

This general acceptability of this explanation is probably due to the fact that it provides some sort of legitimacy to the dowsing process, as it has its origins in the 19th century's scientific community. It is therefore convenient as an explanation.

It is probably fairest to say that, although this is the usual explanation of the dowsing response, it serves only to push the reason for that response back one stage further, where it still awaits a satisfactory explanation.

One important aspect of this is that the connection between the mind and the answer seems to be definitely linked and, as such, that allows for an examination into the nature of mind to perhaps reveal something more about dowsing than is presently acknowledged.

However, as noted in the theories entry (See THEORIES), it is not the only explanation possible, nor is it the only likely explanation possible.

It is highly likely that, as time passes, this explanation will be replaced by something associated with quantum physics (see QUANTUM THEORY) as that has the glitter of both newness and accepted strangeness, both of which would seem to suit dowsing, or appear to make it suitable to non-dowsers.

Until such time, the ideomotor effect will continue to enjoy popularity amongst those dowsers who do not concern themselves unduly with theories and explanations.

❧

Informational Dowsing

For some time, there has been the phrase 'informational dowsing' used as a way of defining one type of dowsing from other types. These other types, presumably, are not concerned with information.

However, as dowsing consists only and solely of asking questions (q.v.) and obtaining answers, then it is clear that the only type of dowsing there is, is informational dowsing.

To attempt to re-define dowsing to make it fit to some other idea is both irrational and unhelpful.

Dowsing is a clearly defined skill. It requires no other definition.

(See INTENTION and HEALING)

❧

Intention

◆Intention is a wonderful thing to have.

◆Without intention, little is ever achieved.

◆Successful intention is based on having specific goals.

◆Intention needs nothing else other than the focus of the human mind.

◆Intention is a mental thing, and nothing else.

Having said all that, there are still those who confuse dowsing with intention. At first, having read the above list, it is hard to see how such a confusion could exist, or how it could be as widespread as it currently is.

The reason for the confusion lies, ultimately, in the poor level of teaching and the lack of thinking, or the unwillingness to think, of those who teach and of those who dowse and continue this confusion.

It has been stated elsewhere (See the Introduction, HEALING, CLEARING), that this confusion exists and reasons for it have been offered. So it is perhaps appropriate that this is the place for a more comprehensive look at the issue.

Dowsing consists of asking questions which the rational mind cannot answer. It therefore is concerned with gathering information. A water dowser, for example, dowses to find the depth, quality and quantity of water underground so that a well might be drilled in the correct spot to meet the requirements of the landowner.

Intention is carried out as a result of a specific belief or willingness to achieve a specific goal. A person could intend, for example, to lose weight and gain fitness by exercising more. If the intention is strong and maintained, then that goal will be achieved. The beliefs underlying that intention are, firstly, that there is a need to attend to fitness and weight. Secondly, that by following such a regime, the need will be met.

Such simple divisions are obvious. However, there are other examples which are, perhaps, not so obvious, unless you are willing to think about them a little more.

Let us take a different dowsing example to better illustrate the issue. A dowser uses the skill to help with a problem she is having. Specifically, the problem she is trying to address is a long-standing one of an inability to focus on work. She has spent much time and effort on various different approaches to resolving this issue, from hypnosis to exercise to trying to follow specific routines to teach herself new habits. None have been successful. Her dowsing indicates that the root cause of the issue is something that happened to her in a past life.

* Note that this is not a physical target. It is not something which can be physically verified in the way that a possible well site can be.

Now, our dowser uses dowsing next to discover which method would work best to resolve this past life issue. The information she gets from this is that a simple and clear statement of intention will do the work for her.

* Note next how the dowsing *information* reveals that intention is required. There is nothing in the dowsing itself which has anything else to do with intention other than revealing that that is the best approach.

Our dowser now makes the statement of intention and focuses her will on clearing the issue of the past life currently affecting her.

* Note this has nothing to do with dowsing.

She next picks up her pendulum to check whether or not the statement has worked. (Let us assume, for the sake of clarity, that she is able to accurately dowse whether or not the issue has gone and not just dowse what she wishes would have happened.) Her dowsing indicates that the issue is now resolved. At work, her focus is much clearer, indicating that the work she did was able to resolve the underlying issue. As such, it is reasonable to assume that her new attitude is the proof necessary, in much the same way that water in a dowsed well site is proof.

Note the sequence of events in the above example:

1. Dowsing to find the root cause (past life)

2. Dowsing to find which method will be most effective (statement of intent)

3. The statement of intent is made

4. Dowsing to check on completion (has the statement worked?)

In other words, there are three dowsing activities and one focused intention separate from them.

Laid out like this, it is obvious that dowsing and intention are not the same, do not occupy the same brain functions but may appear to be simultaneous. So why the confusion?

The answer lies in items 3 and 4 above. If the dowser is using a pendulum, for example, to check on the statement, and has that in motion at the same time as making the statement of intent, waiting for it indicate a 'yes' when the intention has finished, it may look as if the pendulum's movement is somehow connected to the intention. This might be done by an experienced dowser as a way of shortening the process. But, to a new dowser, it is certainly not clear.

From there, it a simple, but illogical, step to assume that the swinging pendulum is responsible for making the intention work.

And, from that point, it is very quick (but, again, illogical and unnecessary) to make even further assumptions that simply rotating the pendulum one way does something different to rotating it in a different way.

Dowsing and intention are both highly useful tools for anyone to master. However, they are two separate tools, not one.

Mingling the two serves to muddy the idea of dowsing as seen from outside the dowsing community, and makes it just as murky inside it. Those who cling to this useless outlook are also helping to present dowsing as a psychic ability, not a natural skill. And that, in turn, leads to discussion being needed on the willingness of those who dowse to invest time and effort to keep sharpening their skill. They will be less and less willing to do so if dowsing is considered as psychic, for, after all, to take the cynical view, if you are psychic, you are born a natural and need no more practice.

If dowsing is to be seen as an actively useful skill and available to all, then the damage being done by this ongoing and pernicious belief is difficult to underestimate.

$\approx$

Intuition

Intuition is said to be at work when information is made available to the individual which was not gathered by any of the five physical senses. The information is seen to appear, sometimes as a whole, directly and all at once, usually without being deliberately asked for.

So, for example, knowing who is phoning you before you see the caller id or pick up the phone is a well-known form of intuition. Another would be to follow an urge to take an unaccustomed or unaccountable action (such as stopping at a green light, or taking a different route) and thus avoiding an accident or meeting someone you needed to see. Sometimes it is just knowing which way to go in a strange town.

However it works for a person, the fact remains that, in some fashion, there was sudden access to previously unknown information.

As such, the skill of dowsing might be considered to be a more focused use of intuition. Instead of waiting and hoping for a random intuitive 'hit' about some aspect of life, dowsing gives a much more structured approach.

Thus, by focusing on a specific goal, asking a carefully formed question (q.v.) and then, in the appropriate dowsing state (q.v.), waiting for the answer, the dowser gains access to information which would not be available to the rational mind.

Indeed, if dowsing is used habitually and regularly, it does appear that there is a significant increase in the natural intuitive ability. Long-term dowsers regularly report that they are better able to intuit situations more accurately. They are able to access the information required more easily and can often gain a deeper insight into issues that dowsing alone would normally provide.

Depending on personal inclinations, the growth of such abilities as clairaudience, clairsentience or clairvoyance (q.v.) have been reported as being strengthened after having practiced long-term dowsing.

Intuition is a well-accepted fact of human life. What is interesting, however, is that the use of dowsing to increase this faculty has not been subject to any serious investigation, when dowsing can give similar results to 'natural' intuition.

∽

INVOLUNTARY MUSCULAR RESPONSE

(See IDEOMOTOR EFFECT)

J

Jurion, Father Jean

Father Jean Jurion (1901 - 1977) is another example of the French Catholic influence upon dowsing (see also RELIGION AND DOWSING, MERMET (ABBÉ) and RADIESTHESIA). In this case, he was introduced to dowsing in 1930, but did not begin to use it until some years later.

There are two aspects of his involvement in dowsing which are of special interest.

First is his development in popularization of medical dowsing. He became so adept at this, incorporating the study of dowsing with an in-depth knowledge of homeopathy, that his success brought him into conflict with authority on numerous occasions, usually because he had been successful in treating a patient when traditional doctors had failed.

The court cases which resulted brought him notoriety and the practice of medical dowsing into greater awareness in France.

The second aspect which is overlooked generally is that he became aware that to be a good dowser does not require specific tools or a set of rituals in order to succeed. He found that the pendulum he liked best was the best pendulum to use, and that attempting to follow what others said was pointless, as there were so many conflicting theories (q.v.) and ideas about dowsing that nothing sensible could be made of them.

This simple and honest approach to dowsing is one which is still, sadly, overlooked today in favor of specific pendulums or colors or rituals by many dowsers.

K

Knowing

Knowing, sometimes written as 'Gnowing' (a reference to a gnosis or esoteric or spiritual knowledge), is often used, in dowsing, to explain the sensation or mode of apprehension of the answers received using this skill.

This word can be used interchangeably with 'intuition' (q.v.). The preference for using the term 'knowing' over intuition by those who use it is presumably to emphasize a closer apprehension of the intuitive message. As the precise mechanics of the dowsing process are unclear, it can be a useful term for dowsers, as long as it does not also infer that the dowser has absolute or incontrovertible knowledge but instead is a way of making clear the nature of how the answer was received, rather than the inherent value of the answer itself.

L

L-rod

One of the most common dowsing instruments, the L-rod is so named because of its shape. The dowser holds the shorter of the two arms and the longer arms are allowed to move freely in response to the ideomotor effect (q.v.) or involuntary muscle response.

These rods come in all different sizes and materials. They are easy to make at home or they can be purchased. Accordingly, the prices vary from nothing to several thousand dollars.

However, there is nothing inherently wonderful or special about any of the rods, as it is the operator, the dowser, who is the reason they work at all. Some dowsers prefer certain lengths or certain materials, but that is purely personal preference and has nothing to do with the efficiency of the tool. (Unless, of course, the dowser believes that to be the case.)

≈

LECHER ANTENNA

This type of dowsing tool has greater popularity in Europe than in America.

The basic design is similar to a y-rod (q.v.), in that it is gripped at the handles and the deflection of the rod is basically the same response.

The main difference is that this tool can be calibrated to respond to specific frequencies, using a sliding scale at the center. See illustration below. It means that the dowser is better able (supposedly) to search for a wide variety of specific energies using this one tool.

However, as the other main tools; the pendulum, l-rod and y-rod, all respond to the dowser's reactions, then the lecher antenna does so as well. Again, it is the dowser who is more important than the tool, and it is true for the lecher antenna as well.

Despite this, there are many users of this tool who will claim that is has a superiority over other types of tools. This has always been the case throughout the history of dowsing. And, again, the key point to note here is that it is the dowser's frame of mind which is the deciding factor here, not the tool itself.

~

LEY LINES

The term 'ley lines' is a confusing one for most people. And it is getting to the point where it is almost impossible to understand what is meant when it is used. It is included in this volume because it is a term which is often used amongst dowsers. The following is an attempt to explain the cause of confusion, not to advocate a 'correct' definition.

It was coined by Alfred Watkins in the UK in the 1920's. He envisaged that Neolithic people (about 10,000 years ago) followed obvious markers on the land, hence the name of his book outlining his idea, *The Old Straight Track*.

According to him, a ley should not be taken as proved with less than four good mark-points. Three good points with several others of less value like cross roads and coinciding tracks may be sufficient. The good mark-points could be any of the following (in descending order of importance) :

1. Mounds (such as burial mounds)

2. Stones (such as monoliths and standing stones)

3. Circular moats

4. Castles

5. Beacons

6. Traditional wells

7. Churches

8. Crossroads of ancient tracks

9. Road alignments (especially over ½ a mile)

10. Fords

11. Tree groups (especially those on ancient named hilltops)

12. Single trees (only if ancient and named)

13. Notches

14. Track junctions

15. Camps

16. Ponds

17. Square moats

Also, a ley should not be longer than 25 miles and they should lie within an arc of 1/4 of a degree.

In other words, the original ley line was something quite specific. Of course, there are plenty of people who disagree with the whole concept, saying that you can pretty much find a ley line anywhere by throwing a straight edge down on a map and seeing what lines up.

To many people today, the term has acquired new meanings. For example, there are those who link the lines to the earth energy grid and suggest that they have a magnetic or some other type of energetic current running through them. Others use this to explain UFOs as following these lines along the earth grid.

Because of the inclusion of standing stones (q.v.) as marker-points, other people have associated the lines with stone circles and asserted that the ancient builders of the circles were aligning them with this energy running through the earth. In other words, the stones are no longer indicators of a possible ley, but an integral aspect of them.

Obviously the later ideas are a far cry from Watkins' original explanation. The difference can be explained by how society has changed. The term 'ley lines' was taken up chiefly by an author, John Michell, in a popular 1970's book, *A View over Atlantis*, which looked at the ancient remnants of Britain through the eyes of a New Age geomancer.

The idea then crossed the Atlantic and the American version, not knowing of the 1920s origins, contained only the energetic aspect. Hence the current emphasis on geomancy, dowsing and the earth energy grid as the American version has fed back across the ocean to the country of origin.

Therefore, you should be aware that when people are talking about ley lines, they might not all be talking about the same thing. Exercise a little caution and decide for yourself whether what they say makes sense to you or not. That's the only thing which matters.

This list gives you some idea of the various meanings associated nowadays with the term;

1. earth radiation
2. earth currents
3. energy lines
4. earth grid
5. prehistoric trade routes
6. holy lines connected with underground streams

However they are termed, it is possible to use dowsing to identify and track ley lines. The easiest method is through the use of l-rods (q.v.) which will indicate the direction more easily than most other tools.

~

Long Pendulum

The long pendulum referred to here is that which T.C. Lethbridge used in his experiments. It is not very well known today and is certainly awkward to use but has an interest all of its own. Thomas Charles (T.C.) Lethbridge was retired from academic life in Cambridge, England, living in Devon, where he started his investigations into dowsing in the 1950's and 1960's. He introduced a neighbor of his, Colin Wilson, the prolific author, to dowsing, who became interested and subsequently wrote about it.

Lethbridge discovered that if a pendulum of a certain length was held over an object (this also applied to concepts such as age, or health or direction), then it would gyrate a certain number of time specific to that object. Thus, for silver, he found that a pendulum of 22 inches in length would rotate 22 times. He therefore declared that the 'rate' for silver was 22/22. Similarly, the same length pendulum would react to lead but would only rotate 16 times, and for the color grey it would only rotate seven times, making their respective rates 22/16 and 22/7.

(This is a variation on the sidereal pendulum (q.v.).)

He explained this behavior as being the response to the thought or focus of the dowser acting somewhat as a ray, and when the pendulum gyrates, it is because the ray has met the obstruction or object of the thought and has been turned back on itself. (See THEORY OF RATES) He also said that the rates were not exact as each ray had a width of two inches. So, the general rate for health was between 31 and 33 inches, therefore he decided to call it 32 inches. Presumably, although he does not say specifically, the pendulum began to rotate at the first measurement and began to degrade at the second.

He also dated coins and other artifacts by allowing a 30 inch pendulum to rotate over them and count the number of turns made, counting back until it stopped. He noted it was mind-numbingly tedious to do this, but appeared to be very accurate. (30 inches was the length Lethbridge set for Age. It was also the length for the color green, the element hydrogen and for water, the moon, sound, and the west (each with a different number of rotations)).

M

Mager Rosette

The Mager Rosette is a disc of eight colors devised originally by a French dowser, Henri Mager, around the beginning of the twentieth century. The colors usually are violet, blue, green, yellow, red, gray, black and white, in that order.

The original use of this color wheel is not certain. Some state that it was devised by Mager in order to test the quality of water, whilst others state that it was more a general way of sorting out which energies were being dowsed. It seems to be true that Mager was interested in researching any correlation that might exist between various substances and certain colors. (See THEORY OF RATES)

According to some sources, the disc should be oriented such that the violet sector is pointing due north, making the other cardinal points, green, red and black. The disc can be of any size. Mager himself had one large enough for him to be able to stand comfortably within each sector. In one of the techniques associated with this color wheel, Mager would place a substance on a particular segment and dowse the cardinal points to see if he had a positive response to it or not. If so, then, presumably, an association was conceived between the two.

That technique is probably rarely used nowadays. Instead, it can be used as a handy way of dowsing the quality of a water sample. The usual meanings of the colors when used for testing water are; Violet: safe to drink; Blue: Drinkable; Green: Copper impurities or mineral impurities in general; Yellow: Salts present, or sulphur; Red: Iron present; Gray: Polluted; Black: Unsafe or dangerous to drink; White: Holy water.

The meanings and associations of the colors can, of course, vary from dowser to dowser depending on use and application.

It is possible, for example, to hold the wheel in one hand while dowsing over various foods, and seeing what happens as you hold each color segment as you dowse. You can then allocate specific colors to specific qualities of the food and then use that same test for any other foods you might purchase.

In energy dowsing, such as following various lines of energy, the color wheel can be used to make associations with various lines to allow for ease of discernment if you should come across more than one. It makes for following one line amongst many much easier.

Although it has been around for over one hundred years, the Mager Rosette seems to be a tool which has not found much support. It is a very simple tool to make for yourself (simply divide a circle into eight segments and color accordingly), and is easily carried. It has many possible uses, but few dowsers seem to know of its existence or of how it could be used.

∾

MAGNETISM, Theory of

Magnetism as a theory to explain dowsing has been somewhat popular and dates back to at least the 19th Century.

An interesting, more modern review of this is given in the magazine *New Scientist* for March 19, 1987. The article suggests that there is merit in the idea, as experiments had shown magnetic anomalies where dowsers had previously located water.

The theory rests upon the idea that in humans, along with many other animals, there are incredibly small magnetic compasses. Such structures have been claimed to have been found in the sinus complex in the front of the skull. Such compasses would react, it is claimed, if they also existed in the muscles of the arms, allowing the tool movement to take place.

If that is not found to be the case (and there seems not to have been much progress in this area since then), the suggestion is that the reaction of the compasses is processed by the subconscious which then makes the muscles move (see also IDEOMOTOR EFFECT).

A Dutch Professor, Solco Tromp, in 1949 also suggested that tiny magnetic changes were detectable by dowsers. Some were, he thought, better at this using a rod of some kind, whilst others were better at using a pendulum, although no reason was given. He also suggested, without apparent testing of the hypothesis, that dowsers were sensitive to very low level infrared radiation. Yves Rocard, Professor of Physics at the Ecole Normale in Paris, also supported the magnetic theory, using a variety of experiments.

Similarly, Dr. Zaboj V. Harvalik, formerly Professor of Physics at the University of Arkansas and advisor to the U.S. Army's Advanced Concept Materials Agency, carried out experiments in the 1960's which noted the extremely low magnetic field variations dowsers could sense.

An interesting review of the various experiments carried out to test dowsing (prior to 1982) can be found in the *Journal of the Society for Psychical Research*, Vol 51, No. 792, October 1982, pp. 343-367.

As with all such theories (q.v.), however, they tend to focus on the strictly practical application of water dowsing, although this magnetic sensitivity could, it is claimed, also help in archeological dowsing as well as in geology and civil engineering.

As ever, it would seem that one theory of dowsing is unlikely to serve to explain all the various applications of the skill. (See also THEORIES)

≈

Map Dowsing

Map dowsing is one of the practical applications of this skill. It straddles the line between the on-site, practical applications and the remote types of dowsing, seeming to fit in neither camp easily. As such, it is sometimes viewed in a more skeptical light than it deserves by non-dowsers.

The maps used in map dowsing do not always have to be drawn accurately or to scale, except in those cases where a precise location is required. Often a map is used to identify an area which is then more closely examined on site. Such would be the case when looking for targets over a large area, as in finding water on a large ranch.

The principle of map dowsing is to reduce the area being searched in a systematic fashion, rather than aimlessly trying to locate a target through hit-and-miss, hunt-and-peck methods.

There are, therefore, two basic approaches to map-dowsing.

The first approach is based on triangulation as used in radio direction finding. Here the search is conducted using whatever tool is comfortable (usually a pendulum (q.v.), although small l-rods (q.v.) are an alternative), a straight edge and a pencil. Holding the straight edge at 90 degrees to an edge so that it projects out across the map, it is then moved along the side of the map until a 'hit' is received (that is, a tool responses indicating that the target has been reached), at which point a line is drawn from the edge across the map. The assumption is that somewhere along that line is the target.

Then the straight edge is used in the same fashion on the next side so that it projects at 90 degrees to the first use. Again, when a 'hit' is registered, another line is drawn and where this line crosses the first is where the target should be.

This procedure can be carried out on the third and fourth edges of the map, if required, to further delineate the target area.

The second approach to map dowsing is to divide the map into four equal quadrants and then dowse in which quadrant the target lies (assuming there is only one target!). That quadrant is then divided again into four equal segments and each is again dowsed for the target location. The corresponding quadrant is then, again, divided into four and so until the remaining area is small enough to be easily identified. (See also CHUNKING DOWN)

For some reason, whenever map dowsing is explained to non-dowsers, they find it hard to accept that it can work. However, if you then ask them to look at a map and identify (as appropriate to the scale) large buildings, major roads, hills and so on, they will readily do so. Pointing out to them that they have done that because they interpreted marks on paper and that they were trained to read them as such goes some way to helping explain that there might be something to the physical drawings which might help to explain the process. Of course, this might have no bearing on the real way map-dowsing works, but it can help to ameliorate outright dismissal of the subject.

∿

MERMET, Abbé

Abbé Alexis Mermet (1866 - 1937) was a French priest in Savoy who experimented with dowsing, especially the pendulum (q.v.). He is credited as being one of the most successful French dowsers (see also AYMAR, BLÉTON and JURION).

He dowsed many wells in his area and also was known for accurately locating missing people. He was himself unsure as to how dowsing worked. Due to his inquisitive nature, he became drawn to the idea that there were aspects to health which were not obvious but which could be ascertained via interrogation using a pendulum.

In 1906 he came to the conclusion that if inanimate objects could be studied through the use of a pendulum, via asking questions, it seemed entirely reasonable to assume that humans and animals could be subjected to the same diagnostic process. As he later wrote in his book, *How I Proceed In The Discovery Of Near Or Distant Water, Metals, Hidden Objects And Illnesses*, "I invented the method of pendular diagnosis."

This was really the beginning of what came to be known as medical dowsing, which other French dowsers helped to popularize (see JURION).

Mermet has a pendulum shape named after him, which is nothing more than a round, usually brass, pendulum, the top of which can be removed so that a witness (q.v.) might be inserted.

Although he did not coin the term 'radiesthesia' (q.v.), he published a popular book, *The Principles And Practice Of Radiesthesia: A Textbook For Practitioners And Students* which helped this idea spread more rapidly.

∼

Mind, The

The role and importance of the mind when dowsing is hard to overestimate. However, it is often the case that such importance is only mentioned in passing when dowsing is taught.

It is important to state clearly that the mind is the single most important, indeed the *only* important aspect of dowsing.

It is in the mind of the dowser that the question is formed and focused upon. It is in the mind of the dowser that the apprehension of the answer occurs, though the tool shows the reaction (see IDEOMOTOR EFFECT). Seasoned dowsers will invariably report that experience makes them less and less reliant on the tool and more susceptible to 'acquiring' the answer in some fashion in their mind as soon as the question has been asked.

More and more scientific research is discovering and confirming the complexity of the mind. Philosophy has long been engaged in examining the mind. All such endeavors serve to bolster the idea that, not only is the mind wondrously complex, but that it is also a continuing source of mystery, exploration and discovery. From the ideas of how beliefs (q.v.) control us from the subconscious, to how the logical and intuitive aspects work together in our lives, the workings of the mind are becoming seemingly more and more complex. Therefore, it would be foolish to attempt to summarize how the mind is involved in dowsing.

All that can be said, with any hope of accuracy, is that the dowser, if she is to be more than merely competent, must learn to appreciate, discipline and develop the mind's role in dowsing.

Thus, being aware of the dowsing state (q.v.) is the first step. Developing an awareness of what that state feels like, how it can change and the various sensations and allied reactions which come to be known when dowsing, are all part of this.

Dowsing, if done rigorously and carefully over time will, it seems from anecdotal evidence, act to change the mind of the dowser. Partly this will come from being carefully logical and analytical in forming questions (q.v.) and partly from allowing the answers to 'arrive.'

The concept of mind also includes thought processes and beliefs, so that involving oneself in dowsing and using it to inquire into the world around, will, almost without question, bring about definite and permanent changes in the the way the world is perceived, to a greater or lesser degree. These new perceptions of the mind will, in turn, bring about changes in the way interactions with the world occur.

There is a very strong case, therefore, for any dowser, especially those new to the skill, to leave tools behind from the beginning and make control of the mind their greatest priority in dowsing; from learning the dowsing state to accessing the answer, it all happens only in the mind.

It is true to say that the art of forming good questions and of allowing the answers to arrive engages both the logical and the rational sides of the brain, and that the continued practice of both of these aspects of dowsing serve to strengthen the mind of the dowser in a way not readily available in other pursuits. (See also WHOLE BRAIN APPROACH)

～

MINERALS

Minerals, in the sense of those substances obtained by mining, have long been the target for dowsing (see AGRICOLA). It is still a common application of dowsing today. There are many reports of the use to which dowsing has been put to discover specific minerals by dowsers in the Russian states. (See BIOPHYSICAL EFFECT)

～

MINING

The earliest obvious depiction of dowsing is for the discovery of metals and metallic ores. (See AGRICOLA)

The need for good sources of metals such as iron and tin meant that any reliable method of locating them was looked on very favorably. Therefore, mines and mining have a long association with dowsing. The dowsers from Germany were famed for their skill and were encouraged to come to England by Queen Elizabeth I, where they established themselves in the West Country. That areas was still the main source of dowsers in the 19th Century.

In France, Jean du Chatelet, Baron du Beausoleil (q.v.), together with his wife, Martine de Bertereau, discovered several hundred profitable mines for the French government.

Russian dowsers (see BIOPHYSICAL EFFECT) of the present time have been documented as using dowsing to locate mineral deposits.

N

Need, Not Greed

'Need not greed' is one of those phrases, like 'It's all good,' which is used mostly without thought.

In dowsing, it is used as a way of holding someone back from profiting from their skill. There is a belief (q.v.) amongst many dowsers that the skill will desert them if they use it for self-profit, such as dowsing for lottery numbers or the winner of a horse race. They are also quick to admonish others who say that they would like to do such things.

This is a viewpoint very typical of the New Age but is not necessarily a useful truth (q.v.).

The concept of greed is a judgment. Usually, it is a judgment on other people and their intentions. For example, making lots of money for what appears to be the sake of making money might be judged to be greedy. But what if the money made was used to fund charitable organizations of some kind? Something impossible without having the money first. Bill Gates made massive amounts of money and was often considered to be very greedy. But, he has donated over $27 billion dollars to charitable causes to date, to help others, and persuaded many other billionaires to do the same.

Judgment in this case was hasty.

The point is, is it ever valid to make such a judgment of others? We can never know the reasons or goals others may have for having money. From forming a charity, to paying for a special vacation or a hospital bill, the possible reasons are never-ending. And, if someone chooses only to make money for the pleasure of making money, that is their choice as well.

When dowsers apply it to themselves and to their own dowsing, there is something different going on. Firstly, they are reinforcing a belief that they may not prosper from their skill. Secondly, they are restricting ways they feel they may use that skill.

For those dowsers who believe that dowsing is a gift granted from God, or something similar, they will believe that its purity or their ability to use it will dissipate if they use it for profit. However, that is just a belief and nothing more.

For the rest, however, they usually repeat it because they've heard it said before from someone they perhaps respect. Maybe it gained reinforcement by them failing to dowse for a profit.

However, if there is any belief at all in the energetic aspect of the world, then it is entirely reasonable to state and believe that either nothing is spiritual or everything is. There can be no middle ground in this belief. You cannot have some spiritual things in the world and choose which those are. If that is so, then money is nothing more than one spiritual aspect of existence and can have no value judgment, good or bad, applied to it.

The 'Need vs Greed' argument is weak. However, that does not automatically mean that every dowser is able to dowse the lottery correctly, find treasure or get the winner of the next big race and make huge amounts of money. Beliefs in the subconscious (q.v.) will still have an effect, as will skill. Not every application of dowsing is equally easy for each dowser to master. That is why some dowsers may be wonderful at locating lost objects and useless at health dowsing, or vice versa.

The reasons for that difference in dowsing success are not clear. It might be down to teaching, to cultural differences, to subconscious beliefs or just lack of confidence in some areas. However, maybe you, the reader, will find that you have a knack for dowsing about money.

~

Negative Green

Negative green is a subject surrounded by a 'cloud of unknowing'.

Much has been written about it accompanied by pseudo-scientific terminology, hearsay and supposition such that it is virtually impossible to have a clearly defined view of the subject which is even approaching objectivity.

Supposedly, negative green is a wavelength, first identified as being present in Egyptian pyramids, which is responsible for the mummification process. It is considered to be problematic if over-exposed to it and that some pendulum shapes (e.g. Karnak - note the Egyptian name!) are transmitters of this wavelength and should, therefore, be dismantled when not in use.

The idea itself came from two men, Chaumery and de Belizal, who are reported as having made the discovery, or developed the theory (it is unclear which), in 1930. It is based on the assumption that any sphere or circle will contain 12 specific energies or different vibrations. Where this developed from is unclear. But it should be noted that, in dowsing, it is very often the case that once an idea is conceived, further dowsing will reinforce that concept.

Having made such a 'discovery,' everything which they subsequently investigated provided further proof of this theory, including, apparently, the reason for the strange tops of the statues on Easter Island!

It would be most instructive if some novice dowsers were given a circle to dowse to see if such a series of energies can be found by them. (This, of course, assumes that there is a definite, objective truth (q.v.) which is available to all: a dubious assumption at the best of times.)

Until such time, it is the author's opinion that the concept of negative green is a weak one at best and spurious at worst.

~

Neutral Swing

The neutral swing is the movement of the pendulum (q.v.) which is neither a Yes or a No. Sometimes it is referred to as the 'ready' motion.

For example, if the pendulum normally moves in a clockwise circle for Yes and counter-clockwise for No, then a neutral swing, in this instance, could be back-and-forth or to-and-fro with respect to the dowser.

In other words, the neutral swing is one which is visually not like either response, and ideally it is also one which allows a swift movement to either response.

Frequently, beginner dowsers will not have a neutral swing, instead holding the pendulum absolutely still and waiting for a motion to begin. This is both tiring and unnecessary. Once both responses are known, then it is a simple matter to decide which motion will become neutral, allowing for faster response times.

Faster response times are very useful for newcomers, as it is difficult to stay in the dowsing state (q.v.) at first, and so the quicker the answer, the better.

O

Odic Force

This is the term Baron Karl von Reichenbach (1788 - 1869) used to describe what he considered as being an energy which flowed through and radiated from everything. He believed that it was able to be perceived by sensitive persons and spent much time devising experiments to this end. The term originated from the god Odin, the chief of the Norse gods.

Among the sensitives he was interested in using were dowsers. Water dowsing, the most usual application of the skill at the time, was, he thought, a reaction to the odic force in the water. (See also THEORIES)

~

Oil Dowsing

Dowsing for oil is one application of the skill. Interestingly, oil-dowsers are sometimes referred to as 'oil-smellers', whereas water dowsers are not usually referred to in the same manner. This is perhaps due to the distinct odor which oil has, rather than any other factor.

~

ON-SITE DOWSING

On-site dowsing is the application of the skill in the location of the target object. So, for example, water dowsing, when carried out on the land where the well is to be located, is a form of on-site dowsing. A search for a lost object in the home, moving from room to room, is another example.

This application is to be compared with remote dowsing (q.v.)

～

ORIGIN Of The Word

Although there might seem to be many strange things about dowsing to a non-dowser, one of the very strangest things of all about it is the word 'dowsing' itself.

It appears to have no real traceable history. In fact, the first occurrence of a word, 'deusing,' in 1691 by John Locke, is considered to be the earliest use of the term. The word appears to come from the West Country in England (the counties of Somerset, Devon and Cornwall), and Locke's spelling of it might be his attempt to reproduce how it was (and still is) spoken. There is nothing discovered so far, however, which is conclusive about it.

It seems that the word suddenly sprang into use around 1700 for no obvious reason at all! The activity of dowsing has a longer history, and the tools or the methods used also had names. But the activity itself, apparently, was not known by its present name until the end of the seventeenth century, at least in English-speaking countries.

～

OVERGROUND WAVES

Overground waves are offered by some dowsers as being dowseable phenomena. These are more commonly thought to be associated with standing stones (q.v.) or other similar monuments.

Naturally, the precise nature of these waves does not seem to correspond to the usual concepts as preferred by physicists who are thinking in terms of electromagnetic radiation.

What these waves may be, or how they come to be propagated, is open to experimentation and discovery. Nevertheless, there are many dowsers who profess an ability to follow such waves over many miles.

Some may speak of them in much the same way as classical physics does, in that they emanate across the land, above ground and are deflected or absorbed or otherwise affected by other physical objects.

Others, however, see them as following paths which wind around and amongst physical objects, rather than following straight lines.

Both cases might be equally true and may, in that case, represent two different types of waves.

Nevertheless, the origin, propagation and radiation of such phenomena remains to be fully explained. At such time, presumably, they will be able to be fitted into the accepted scientific framework.

P

Paramelle

Abbé Paramelle (b. 1790) is of interest here in that he was immensely prolific at siting water wells. However, the interest is not in that he was successful about 95% of the time, but that he did not use dowsing to do so. In fact, he said that dowsing tools did not work for him. Why, then, is he included in this volume?

The answer to that lies in the way he did discover wells. He spent nine months a year, working six days a week at this, and independent assessment gives something like 10,000 wells sited (with the above 95% success rate).

He claimed that by studying the land he could, with great speed, give a precise indication of the location of the well and also provide accurate figures of the depth and yield. (These figures were born out when the well was dug.) Further, he claimed that he could train anyone else in the space of a few months to be just as expert as himself in this. The fact that no student of his has come to notice is probably proof that his was an unusual expression of an ability to interpret the land, in much the same way that Mozart expressed an unusual ability in musical composition.

His method of siting wells is close to how skeptics (see SKEPTICISM) claim that all well sitings by dowsers are accomplished: subconscious or conscious reading of the landscape. While it is certainly true that having a wealth of experience such as Paramelle showed will certainly help, the influence of the subconscious (q.v.) beyond 'seeing' the land should not be overlooked.

Now, while it is unlikely that many modern water dowsers could claim anywhere near the field experience of Paramelle, it is entirely possible that the subconscious or unconscious aspects of the dowser's mind (q.v.) play a vital role in providing extra data when dowsing.

Paramelle was undoubtedly gifted in the way he could 'read' the landscape. This 'unconscious' reading of landforms may go some way to explaining why modern tests of dowsers show no more than chance results. The tests are artificial and the pipes over which the dowsers are asked to dowse bear no relation to the natural process of dowsing.

Where Paramelle was expert at reading the land without resorting to the use of tools, there is no reason not to suppose that the most successful of water dowsers have that same latent ability in some form which, when allied to the use of a tool, gives them a greater than average facility.

Then again, it is reasonable also to suggest that Paramelle *was* dowsing, albeit without tools, and able to 'see' the correct well location by focusing on what he was after.

～

Past, Dowsing The

See ARCHEOLOGICAL DOWSING and PAST LIVES

～

Past Lives

For some, this subject makes no sense, and for others it is charged with meaning. A belief in reincarnation or in somehow passing information (outside of the usual DNA) through generations is a prerequisite for this subject to make any sense. (Although a brief review of the present state of research into epigenetics will go some way to offer support to the basic claims as made in the first point (below).)

Assuming the belief in past lives exists, then their influence, in dowsing terms, is considered to be one or other (possibly both) of the following.

1) Having lived and experienced a past life, there may well have been a trauma in that life sufficiently strong to have been passed down. The remnants, or echoes, of such a trauma are still resonating in the subconscious mind and can, accordingly, influence this present life. Thus, for example, if, in a past life, there was death by drowning, it is likely or possible that a fear of water still exists and would make dowsing about or for it a problematic affair. This would be because the mind would not want to re-visit the incident again and would, therefore, throw the results off wherever the target was concerned with finding water.

2) The other view of past lives, with specific regard to dowsing, is that, if one or any of them is having any influence on the present life, then the root issue is believed to be within the subconscious (q.v.). The use of dowsing can bypass the conscious mind and directly engage with the subconscious and discover the underlying issues. Once achieved, the issues can be cleared and the effects of the past therefore will no longer affect the present life.

This second aspect, the discovery of past lives through dowsing, is probably the more widely known and has formed an integral part in several current healing modalities.

However, the first example is one which should also be considered by any dowser facing problems or issues in one or more aspects of their dowsing.

Most dowsers do, in fact, have a belief in past lives. Some come to dowsing already convinced of the fact, whilst others are persuaded through the course of their dowsing experiences.

~

Pendulum

The pendulum is probably the most widely used of all dowsing tools. As such, there are seemingly limitless variations on what is essentially a weight which is suspended on a thread, string or similar, and allowed to swing freely. It became more widely used at the end of the nineteenth century, being popularized by mainly French dowsers such as Abbé Mermet (q.v.). There are isolated examples of pendulums being used in dowsing prior to that, but nothing of note to suggest that it was in any way a popular or usual tool. It gained further popularity in the 1920's when it was given a variety of names. (See SIDEREAL PENDULUM)

Wood, metal and precious or semi-precious stones are the most common varieties. Faced with such a wide range of choices, the beginner dowser tends to accrue a selection, before, after a period of time, limiting their choice to one or two.

There is nothing inherently better or worse about any pendulum, except how the dowser regards it. (See JURION, FATHER JEAN)

Using a pendulum effectively requires that the relationship between the weight of the pendulum and the length of the string, chain or whatever be taken into consideration.

What this means practically is that, for a heavier weight, which will move more slowly, the length should be longer than for a lighter weight, which will be far more responsive on a shorter length. Here, a light weight would be anything around one to two ounces, whilst a heavier weight would be four or five ounces.

One problem many new dowsers create for themselves is to have a lightweight pendulum (usually their first tool), on a very long length of chain and to hold it still waiting for a movement to occur.

A lightweight pendulum, such as the crystal ones seen for sale in most shops, need only have a very short length indeed, around an inch or so in length. Heavier ones would need to adjust the length to something nearer five or six inches. You will get a feel for the right length because the pendulum will simply 'feel' easier, freer or more receptive. There are some complex maths available for those who want to discover the 'correct' length for their pendulum, but holding it with a short chain between the thumb and forefinger (the easiest and most natural method) and making minor adjustments until the 'feel' changes and the movement becomes smooth is much the easiest approach.

Obviously, the 'right' pendulum for you will be according to your needs. If you will be walking and holding a pendulum, then a heavier one will be more reliable. A lighter one will be ideal for working at a table over a map, for example. Such different uses explain why virtually all dowsers will accumulate a variety of pendulums for varying tasks or circumstances (apart from the visual appeal).

The pendulum is most effective (given that the length is correct), when it is in motion before the question is posed. The swing, which is a neutral swing, being neither a 'yes' or a 'no' swing, can then rapidly and easily move to either the 'yes' or 'no' response. This automatically assumes that the dowser is aware of what is a neutral swing. (See PROGRAMMING)

The movements of the pendulum can change over time. This is probably due to the familiarity of the dowser with the pendulum allowing for differing movements. Let us say that the 'yes' response is a clockwise (seen from above) circling. After time, it might change to a straight to and fro movement with regard to the body of the dowser. That is not a problem. In fact, anecdotally, it appears to happen to a large percentage of dowsers.

Sometimes, an entirely new movement is made apparent. This can often cause confusion. The original 'yes' and 'no' movements remain the same, but then a new one manifests.

The simplest way of dealing with this situation (which, again, anecdotally appears widespread amongst dowsers who are just coming out of the 'newbie' label) is to ask a series of questions as to what the new movement means. After all, the 'yes' and 'no' responses are still the same. Some of the answers which have been noted about a new movement include that it could indicate 'maybe', 'unclear question', 'not able to answer this question', 'not at this time', 'poor question', 'really strong yes' and 'really strong no.'

An indication of some of the sloppy thinking which can enter into dowsing is the way some people refer to their pendulum (or other tool) by saying something like, 'My pendulum told me so-and-so,' as if it were somehow alive and able to communicate. What in effect is happening at such times is that the tool is being given the power to answer questions when, instead, it is the dowser who is answering the questions, by using the tool to indicate the answer. It may seem a minor quibble and one which could be explained as a shorthand for how the answer was obtained, but such thinking only serves to remove the dowser from the dowsing skill and place it firmly and wrongly in the hands of the tool. It is always the dowser who provides the answer.

~

Pendulum Healing

See HEALING

~

Permission

Permission is easily one of the most confused aspects of dowsing, although it need not be if some very simple rules are kept in mind.

Permission is also something which has become more prevalent over, say, the last 40 years. Prior to that, there is scant mention of it in the literature. Presumably this is because dowsers were not involving themselves in exercises which interfered with the rights or free-will or privacy (however it is expressed) of others. A more practical approach to the subject meant that there was little need to think of permission as a necessary first step.

First, however, it is worth spending some time on one type of permission which has grown considerably over the last generation or so; that of asking permission to dowse in general.

The phrase most usually taught is, 'May I?, Can I?, Should I?' This is particularly prevalent in the United States where it has a firm foothold amongst dowsers. The reason for this is that, originally, it was used by a dowser, Sig Lonegren, in his book, *Spiritual Dowsing*, and he suggested that it be used by beginner dowsers as a way of tuning in to a target.

However, as such things happen, the phrase was taken up and adopted by many other dowsers, for reasons which are not entirely clear, and became a standard part of teaching dowsing, thus spreading the concept of permission far and wide.

There are several issues here which need examining in order to clarify the problem.

First amongst them is the idea that Sig Lonegren's very specific statement about beginners very quickly became a habit for all dowsers to use in preparation for dowsing about anything at all.

Secondarily, this act of asking permission became a short-circuit to a dowser dowsing about anyone at any time.

Thirdly, and one of the biggest problems, is, precisely what is being asked of whom in this statement? Because Sig never re-phrased or chose to define the phrase, it has been commandeered by anyone who had an opinion. The resulting mess is that it is possible to hear dowsers saying that this statement is contacting one's High Self (q.v.), or the Dowsing System (whatever that might mean to the person), or to some unspecified arbiter of dowsing ethics who resides….somewhere.

In brief, by asking these questions, the dowser is abdicating from personal consideration and ethics and handing the decision over to some unspecified source, thus diminishing their own power by denying it to themselves at the same time as refusing to consider the ethical aspects of their own dowsing.

Dowsing, when done well, means that any question may be asked about any time or place or person. That freedom of operation does not automatically mean that every dowser is entitled to, or should engage in, dowsing about another person, place or event for which they have no ethical reason to intrude. For it *is* an intrusion, on an energetic level. Although nobody as yet knows for certain how dowsing works, it is safe to assume that there is some sort of connection at some level between the dowser and the object of inquiry.

Ethics (q.v.) is a wide-ranging subject, a major component of philosophical studies and is to be found in all professional bodies as part of their code of practice. It does, therefore, play a major part in society, in one way or another.

If a dowser, then, asks, for example, the 'May I?, Can I?, Should I?' question, or something like it, the ethical aspect of involvement in something not personal and private to that dowser is being handed over, in some fashion, to another, unknown body. The dowser has, effectively abdicated personal responsibility for any subsequent decisions or questions.

Whilst there are those dowsers who do use the statement and get a negative answer, and do not subsequently dowse, there are plenty of others who use it as an excuse to follow their own interests and use it as a cover for their own lack of ethical considerations.

Quite simply, ethical dowsing means that, if you want to dowse about someone, then ask them directly. Don't excuse yourself by asking their High Self. Don't assume they won't mind. Don't do anything unless and until they specifically give you permission to dowse about them. Handing that responsibility off to an unknown source does not mean you can continue, or you are enlightened, or that you know better. Dowsing about someone else is like entering into their home uninvited. You would not wish that for yourself, and it is common manners, if nothing else, to not do it to others.

Permission in dowsing means exactly and precisely that; gaining permission from the person involved, directly and without an intermediary in whatever form. The only times that would be different would be if you were dowsing about a young child and the parent had to give express permission, as they would for their animal companion. In both cases, where they are unable to speak directly, the next action would be to ask the child or animal themselves if they would mind you dowsing about them.

In fairness to Sig, it is important to point out that later on in his book, he is very specific about permission. As he was the unwitting cause of the three questions, it is worth quoting what he says to balance it out:

"…Let us consider two very important notions. The first is one which is totally ignored by many dowsers: the necessity of permission…. You wouldn't go into someone's house without their consent. Why should you attempt to work with the energies in and around their bode without their permission as well?" And it is vital to note that Sig was speaking only of helping people. Not of interfering with their free will or anything else.

If you cannot gain permission from the person involved, or from a parent or guardian, then you do not have permission to dowse. It is that simple. Muddying the waters with vague phrasing and uncertain sources of answers does nobody any help at all and makes any dowser who disregards such actions look and act like an intrusive busybody and, by association, taints dowsing as the practice of unrestrained gossips and meddlers.

Finally, it is important to demolish another aspect of this whole permission thing, and that is the excuse (for it is nothing more than that) that one's dowsing is only for the highest or greatest good.

The concept of 'greatest good' is one fraught with difficulty but is never, ever addressed as such by those who use it to excuse their actions and to hide their egotistical desire to interfere behind.

Firstly, if the concept of 'highest' good or 'greatest' good is admitted, then, logically, one cannot know what that could possibly be. It is easy to argue for one's own good and even defend that logically. But to whom and in what way does the label 'greatest' or 'highest' apply?

It could very well be that the greatest good of any virulent disease lies in the making of the cure and other medical advances. But, for those who die from it, it would be hard to convince them or their families of any greater good.

In other words, such concepts are impossible to define in any absolute fashion which could be agreed upon. The greatest mistake dowsers commit when using this statement is the underlying, unspoken assumption that the 'good' will be obvious (hopefully, at least, to the dowser). It is never ever conceived that a 'good' might be, in fact, viewed as anything but, in the short term.

As noted earlier, this useless and ill-conceived term is nearly always used as an excuse to avoid getting permission and to act as justification for an ego-driven interference into affairs which are not the concern of the dowser. It should be stated loudly and clearly that the term cannot ever be defined and does not automatically mean something 'nice' (as in a value judgment of the outcome) is going to happen, even in the short term.

There is a certain sadness in realizing that such sloppy thinking, poor dowsing and ego-driven selection of targets justified by the use of this meaningless phrase will still continue to blight the view (and possible wider acceptance) of dowsing as a whole.

∽

PERSONAL GROWTH

Many dowsers are attracted to using dowsing for their own personal growth. This comes about through the natural quest for self-knowledge and self-awareness which we all experience to one degree or another. However, when a dowser realizes that he or she has the ability to ask any question (q.v.) at all (assuming it is well-formed), then there is a general tendency to use dowsing to help reveal and understand previously hidden aspects of their personality.

And it is certainly true the use of dowsing in this area can help you to achieve results. The reason for saying this is that, in most cases, personal growth is based on the idea that there is some aspect of your life which you wish to change but are finding it hard to do so without engaging in some routines or exercises outside the normal state of affairs.

Why some things are harder to change than others can, of course, vary from individual to individual. But it is probably true to say that the more stubborn issues are there because of some hidden blocks. Those blocks are usually to be found in the subconscious (q.v.).

While there are some techniques which might work, such as affirmations, meditation and the like, the true cause of the issue, the actual blocks themselves, are, of course hidden. However, dowsing can be used to access the subconscious and discover what needs to be addressed and how it can be dealt with. (See BELIEFS)

This is because dowsing allows direct access to the subconscious. Hypnosis would also access this area, but dowsing is easier, quicker, cheaper and as just as effective, if carried out carefully.

Once the specific block has been identified, then dowsing can also be used to discover which would be the most effective method or combination of methods you could use to deal with it.

In other words, dowsing allows you to shortcut the process of investigating, cataloging and dealing with the various unconscious issues you might be facing at any one time. And that, of course, allows you to reach your personal growth goals more quickly.

Any time you are wishing to make a change in your life, to improve it, and you find that there is resistance or an inability to maintain the required change, then the use of dowsing will help you to zero in on the pertinent issues and resolve them more quickly than a hit or miss approach would provide.

∾

Physical Effects On The Person

The physical effects of dowsing on the person are most usually associated with dowsing for water. Some of the noted effects are weakness, fainting, staggering and dizziness. The precise nature of these effects are, of course, open to interpretation, as is the reason for them. However, they have been so widely reported over many years and in numerous societies as to preclude any obvious means of transmitting such tendencies through the written to spoken word.

Many of these experiences were noted by Professor Barrett in his exhaustive study of dowsing and gathered into one volume as *The Credibility of Dowsing*.

(See also BLÉTON)

≈

VON POHL

Von Pohl, or, to give him his full name and title, Gustav Freiherr von Pohl (b. 1873) (the term 'Freiherr' is equivalent to 'Baron'), was a dowser with a keen interest in identifying the reasons for poor health. He was a dowser and had developed a theory that some deaths were caused by influences in the earth. He originally sought out fault lines as he believed that they were the cause. However, this line of inquiry drew a blank.

He was then encouraged to consider that, perhaps, it might be something else instead. This 'something' he called energy currents emanating from underground water veins. The problem was to find a site which would provide him with sufficient opportunity to prove his theory.

He eventually settled on the town of Vilsbiburg (q.v.), in Bavaria. The reason for this selection was that, although small, it had suffered a tremendously high death rate from cancer. In the previous ten years, there had been 54 deaths from this disease. The town, when von Pohl visited, had 3,300 people living in 565 houses and 900 apartments. 42 of the houses had a history of seven deaths from cancer.

The concept of Cancer Houses (places where deaths from cancer were more prevalent) was well-known, but there was no existing theory as to why these places were so prone to the disease.

In order to avoid accusations of bias or poor procedure, von Pohl gained permission to dowse in and around the town, but only in the accompaniment of a police officer who ensured that he spoke to no-one, and that he did not enter any dwelling.

In January of 1929, from the 13th to the 19th he dowsed around the town, marking his findings on a map. At the same time, and without his knowledge, the town's medical officer, Herr Bernhuber, marked on a similar map each location of a cancer death.

When the two maps were compared, each of the deaths was found to have occurred in beds exactly over or upon a line of energy which von Pohl had traced.

The results were dismissed by many as being the result of fraud or as just plain nonsense. In order to refute such claims, the town of Grafenau, also in Bavaria, was visited in the following year. This choice was dictated by the fact that it had one of the lowest cancer deaths. The same procedure was followed here as in Vilsbiburg with the same results. All cancer deaths, for 17 years (the length of time records had been kept) were found to be directly over strong underground water veins.

Returning to Vilsbiburg 18 months after his original survey, it was found that the subsequent ten deaths from cancer had occurred, as all the previous ones had, over the strong veins dowsed by von Pohl.

It is doubtful whether anything would have changed even with these results. However, in June 1930, von Pohl presented them to a medical conference in Munich and they were published in July 1930 in the *Journal of Cancer Research*. This gave them a much wider audience, but it was not until after World War Two that further research was carried out in detail.

He published his experiences in a book, *Earth Currents as Pathogenic Agents for Illness and the Development of Cancer*.

What makes these results important in this subject is that they provided the first proof that something which could not be seen *but which could be dowsed for*, could have a serious effect on health. Vilsbiburg and von Pohl marks the beginning of the investigation of earth energies, particularly by dowsing, which has, in turn, developed into specialties such as geopathic stress (q.v) investigation, space clearing (q.v.) and aspects of baubiologie (q.v.).

∽

POLARITY

Polarity in this case refers to the polarity of the human body. It is the contention of most dowsers that this very weak field can be easily 'flipped' and that such a switch in polarity is responsible for the dowser obtaining wrong answers. Specifically, it is thought that such a polarity shift will mean that the normal 'yes' response becomes 'no' and vice versa. (See SWITCHING)

The switching of the polarity is thought to be caused by standing in an area of geopathic stress (q.v.) or by the dowser having an emotional response (usually fearful) associated with the target.

In such cases, the polarity is said to be restored by performing one of the following actions:

1. Taking the first two fingers of the right hand and sweeping them across the forehead from right to left several times while stating the intention to restore the polarity to its right and perfect function.

2. Forming a fist and tapping it lightly against the breastbone (in the area of the thymus - hence the name 'Thymus Thump' for this procedure) while stating the intention to restore the polarity to its right and perfect function.

3. Rubbing vigorously on the acupuncture points known as the K27's (on the kidney meridian, in the hollow just beneath the collar bone on each side of the body) while making the same statement as in point 2, above.

Applying one of the three methods above does make the dowsing response go back to normal. In the few cases where it does not appear to do so, then one of the methods to resolve switching will work.

It would appear that the human electromagnetic field is far from being as simple as dowsers would like it to be. It is very, very weak indeed (about one million times weaker than the Earth's magnetic field) and consists of a number of fields emanating from cells, nerves, the brain and the heart, to name just a few. Superconducting Quantum Interference Devices (SQUIDS) are extremely sensitive machines which can measure these very weak magnetic and electrical fields. One or more of these fields may well be responsible for the reversed actions of the dowser.

It should not be ruled out that the protocols outlined above work because the dowser expects them to work, not because there is any proof of reversed polarity. In which case, this explanation is merely one of convenience in explaining a problem which occurs sometimes amongst dowsers and might, in fact, have no basis in fact.

∾

Prayer

See PROTECTION

～

Programming

Programming is the term given to a number of processes in dowsing. The most usual application of the term is when a dowser decides upon a certain action or motion of the tool and makes the tool move in the required way a number of times until satisfied that the tool will always respond in that fashion in the future. For example, when using a pendulum, the dowser might prefer that the movement of the tool to indicate a 'yes' response will be a clockwise motion and that a 'no' response will be a counter-clockwise motion. For each, she will deliberately make the pendulum move in the required direction while impressing on herself that 'this is the movement for 'yes' (or 'no', as appropriate) until satisfied that the tool will always respond in a clockwise movement for 'yes' and a counter-clockwise movement for 'no.'

In effect, what is happening in such a scenario is that the dowser's muscle reactions are being programmed into the subconscious so that the movement of the tool may be relied upon in the future.

A variation of this type of programming would be where the dowser makes it quite clear (again, to the subconscious (q.v.)) that when a specific set of circumstances occurs, then the tool should react in a different way. So, for example, upon encountering an electro-magnetic field strong enough to have a negative effect on the health of the dowser, the pendulum should move in a diagonal, instead of the usual circular motion.

Another form of programming in dowsing is when the dowser takes a long and very detailed question or circumstance and reduces it down to a very short and simple question. For example, if dowsing about the health of an animal companion, the dowser would want to know if the animal should be taken to the vet only if the following conditions are met:

•The condition cannot be treated by the dowser or

•The condition will not resolve itself favorably without further harm to the animal

•The dowser does not have access to the necessary medications, supplements, healing modalities or other treatments necessary for full recovery

Instead of asking this long question, which might also be at an emotional time and some parts of the question would therefore be likely to be missed, the dowser programs herself that when she asks, 'Should I take this animal to the vet?', the preceding precise and detailed series of questions are the ones which the answer relates to.

A variation of this type of programming occurs when the dowser has a belief that, in order to dowse with confidence and accuracy, a certain sequence of things has to occur. It might be that she wishes herself to be cleared of any energies which might be interfering with her dowsing, and that she also wishes to be grounded and in the dowsing state (q.v.) before proceeding. Having done these things one at a time for all the times she has dowsed, she now feels confident that, by stating something like, 'Prepare to dowse,' her system knows exactly what to do and in what order to be ready. Thus, she is programming her subconscious and conscious mind to go through the various steps she considers necessary.

The problem with this variation is that she is in danger of making the whole process a ritual which loses efficacy over time without her realizing it. This is similar to the problems surrounding permission (q.v.).

There is also another type of programming which relates to dowsing and which should not be overlooked. Here, the programming can be considered cultural or social in origin. As such, the dowser may have been programmed to believe that a problem being investigated can only be attributable to one or two causes. Such programming would then it make it very difficult to allow that there could be any other cause, thus making the dowser less effective.

This type of programming tends to be the most pernicious and difficult to undo, as it requires a level of self-awareness which is not usual. However, it is possible to overcome this by consciously allowing oneself to access the most appropriate or helpful answer, whether or not it is in accord with one's beliefs (q.v.).

≈

Projection

The projection of some aspect of the dowser has been offered as one possible explanation of distance dowsing.

It is sometimes thought that the aura might be projected in some fashion and that there is some form of interaction which occurs which allows information to be acquired.

However, it is possible that a much older idea could also be involved. It is outlined in Claude Lecouteux's book, *Witches, Werewolves and Fairies: Shapeshifters and Astral Doubles in the Middle Ages.* He points out that very ancient traditions, across a range of societies, point to the concept that the physical body has three souls and that one of them is capable of traveling outside of the physical body. His research contains many references to such events and he stresses that an astral double is entirely conceivable. If this is so, then this might also be a possible explanation of how information is gathered at a distance in some cases. (See REMOTE DOWSING)

≈

Proof

Proof of dowsing is often thought of as the Holy Grail by dowsers in that they believe it exists, but any proof offered so far is not recognized by skeptics.

The problem of proof lies in ascertaining what can actually be accepted as proof by those who mistrust dowsing and dowsers. The most commonly offered form of proof is that of finding water through dowsing. However, this is usually repudiated because the counter-argument states that water is easily accessible pretty much anywhere underground and that dowsing is not necessary to find a water source. This is the reason for then trying to control the dowser's environment through burying pipes in the ground and asking one or more dowsers to a) find them, and/or, b) report on whether water is flowing through them at any given time.

Even should one series of experiments be carried out which seem to 'prove' dowsing is valid, it would require many more experiments to be carried out before any consensus could be agreed upon. That could well take a very long time indeed.

From the many and varied investigations into dowsing having been carried out over the years, it would seem that the most likely proof will not be in the form of one or two experiments, but rather due to prolonged exposure to dowsing (usually water dowsing, but not necessarily), which would tend to wear down inherent objections.

But such proof would rely on an active dowser being willing and able to be criticized, and a researcher willing and able to spend a long period of time in close proximity to the dowser and also willing to exercise some self-restraint in not dismissing any or all of what the dowser does.

Of course, scientists would object greatly to any such program from the start.

It seems, then, that obtaining proof is not yet about to happen.

(See SCIENCE AND DOWSING, SKEPTICISM and TRUTH)

~

PROTECTION

Protection as a concept comes in two forms. First is the idea that some form of protection is necessary whenever dowsing takes place. The second form is that protection is sometimes necessary when dowsing about certain aspects of the world.

For the first form, it is the belief (q.v.) of some dowsers that there is some unexplained esoteric aspect to the whole process and that by asking questions in the usual way they are somehow opening themselves up to unknown forces or interferences in the universe which will either confuse their answers or cause them harm. Usually, such beliefs arise from a dualistic view of the world (see DUALISM) and are less than helpful, as they act to restrict what the dowser believes is possible or safe, or both. Chief amongst the responses to this belief is prayer, usually in the form of asking for protection provided by either a specific entity such as Archangel Michael, or generically from guides or some such which are supposed to have one's best interest at heart.

The second form of protection, that of self-protection against that which could be harmful to the dowser, arises from a healthy regard for one's own safety and is to be commended. When a dowser becomes involved in such activities as space clearing (q.v.) there is a very good chance that, at some point, inimical energies of one type or another will be encountered. Debating the effects of such things as curses, aliens, or entities is irrelevant only because this is not the forum for such to take place. It is, however, entirely reasonable to point out that many of those involved in space clearing have come across cases where there was a significant health risk involved or that whatever was being the subject of the clearing was able to exert an effect on the dowser such that the dowsing itself was compromised.

In this latter case, outside influence on the dowser is real and protection against it is necessary. But, it should be stressed, that such circumstances are nearly always confined to space clearing or its variants where the dowser deliberately and consciously engages with such energies, and protection in these cases is not a ritual but tailored to each individual instance.

～

Psychics & Dowsing

It is thought, by some people, that dowsing is a psychic ability akin to tarot reading or channeling (q.v.). The reason for this erroneous belief is that the answers which psychics get cannot be readily explained, just as dowsing cannot be readily explained.

However, dowsing is really a simple skill which is a natural part of human nature. While it could be argued that everyone can channel or read tarot cards, the difference is that such activities do not have a specific focus or goal, as dowsing does.

For a psychic, the important aspect of whatever method being used, is to 'get' the message in some fashion. It could be that a certain sequence of tarot cards triggers a meaning for the reader, as do certain combinations of symbols with regard to what has been asked. Yet, such activities are markedly different from dowsing for one specific reason.

In dowsing, nothing happens unless and until a (hopefully precise) question (q.v.) is asked which can only be answered by either a 'yes' or a 'no'.

In other words, the activity of dowsing is predicated upon the idea that there is a very precise question which has one of two answers. (See BINARY NATURE OF DOWSING)

In psychic activities, the questions are far more general and vague and the answers are of a similar nature: more wide-ranging and holistic than any dowsing answer would be. Also, there are gifted psychics who are able to 'tune in' to their ability with far greater ease than others. It becomes more of an art than anything else (although the element of skill is recognized).

In dowsing, because it is a skill only, it can be taught and be practiced until proficiency is gained.

Psychics, as noted above, are frequently born, not made. Dowsers, however, can be trained. Everyone is capable of dowsing, which is not true of having and using psychic abilities.

A psychic may receive information in a variety of ways; seeing a scene playing out, hearing something, feeling something and so on. These messages can often be detailed or annoyingly vague. They can convey a great deal of information or nothing more than a general feeling of what to do or how to act.

Dowsing, however, receives specific information directly relevant to the question. However, this is not to say that dowsers do not or cannot receive such types of information as psychics do. Indeed, seasoned dowsers usually find that their intuitive skills improve as their dowsing improves, so that the intuitive 'hits' they receive act as highly useful *additional* information to the dowsed answer. But the central core of dowsing is the precise nature of the answer. Any subsequent embellishment does not alter that fact.

In brief, then, dowsing is different from psychic abilities due to the precise nature of the activity, which can be learned and demonstrated by virtually everyone. Using another analogy to help explain the difference; psychics cast their nets and haul in a lot of information, both pertinent and indirectly associated with the query, whereas dowsers use a harpoon to gather precisely the information required as posed by the question.

Q

Quantum Theory

In the never-ending search for the definitive theory which will explain dowsing, the lure of quantum physics has proven to be very strong indeed.

The basic strangeness of quantum physics has allowed it to become the 'go to' explanation for the dowsing phenomenon. Concepts such as non-locality and quantum entanglement have been used as an explanation of how answers are arrived at.

The use of the word 'quantum' in many areas outside of physics is supposed to show either that the subject under discussion is very advanced or difficult to express simply, or, more usually, that there is something about it which cannot be explained using careful, rational analysis. It is therefore considered to be esoteric and not amenable to such analysis. This is the usual way it is used with reference to dowsing.

It does not actually explain anything very well, but does hint at the idea that some aspects of dowsing are possibly strange and not able to be explained or demonstrated using the classical physical model.

This may well be correct, but simply throwing the term 'quantum' at anything which is hard to explain or describe well is not a particularly helpful approach if the idea is to make dowsing more widely accessible, or, at the very least, understandable.

To put this tendency into a clearer perspective, it is informative to examine how radium and x-rays were used in marketing at the beginning of the 20th Century. Such terms were bandied about and used to explain why one product was better than the rest with little regard to either truth or safety!

~

Questions

Questions are at the very heart of dowsing. A well-formed question, together with the correct dowsing state (q.v.) will invariably provide better results than a creating a hastily drawn up question and then immediately turning to the tool for an answer.

Although the concept of good dowsing questions seems to be widely appreciated, it does not seem to be so well applied. The reasons for that are, probably, the familiar ones of poor teaching and lack of interest in the preliminaries and an eagerness to simply 'get an answer.'

Given that experienced and practiced dowsers all readily acknowledge the importance of solid questions, there has been a surprising lack of well-written, detailed works on the subject. Those which make up the bulk of available material are usually found to be repeating a shortlist of points and then providing a very limited number of examples of dubious value. The most detailed work in this area is, without doubt, that of Maggie Percy, whose book *Ask The Right Question,* should probably be provided to every student of dowsing in order to get them on the right track from the very start of their dowsing careers. At well over 100 pages, there really is nothing to compare it with either in terms of clarity of explanation or number and variety of examples.

However, this volume does not have the ability to enter into that level of detail. Nevertheless, what follows is an attempt to be as succinct as possible without burying the main points beneath unnecessary explanations or skimming too shallowly so that important aspects are overlooked.

To begin, it is important to remember that dowsing consists solely of searching for answers. It is nothing else, no matter how seductive other definitions might appear at first. A dowser dowses to find an answer. And that answer is, therefore, the result of asking a question. Even a water dowser, who apparently to the uneducated eye is simply wandering around waiting for a reaction of the tool when over water, even he or she will not begin until a properly framed question is asked and the dowsing state entered into.

Therefore, it can be seen that dowsing cannot and does not happen unless and until a question is asked and there is a reason to pick up the tool. Anything which does not take this vital first step into account is not dowsing.

Assuming, therefore, that there is a general idea for an enquiry in mind, the next step is to create a well-formed question. The term 'well-formed' is used advisedly to emphasize that the question should be constructed with care; that is, not composed quickly and superficially, but ensuring all the proper and relevant aspects of the subject of the enquiry are both made clear and accounted for accurately and without ambiguity.

When stated in this manner, it can seem to be a somewhat daunting exercise. However, it is important to bear in mind that, with practice, the formulation of questions becomes much, much easier and quicker and that the time spent initially on them will inevitably lead more quickly to greater accuracy as well as a gain in the overall appreciation and understanding of the true nature of dowsing.

As a general rule, a question should provide the dowser with useful information; that is, information which will be of direct benefit and, often, allow the dowser to move on to a more detailed examination of the subject, if not supply the full (and useful) answer. But, although all questions will provide answers, it is not always the case that the answers are as useful as they could be. Thus it is important to remember that the more detailed and specific the question is, the more useful the resulting answer will be.

There are a very few, simple guidelines which will aid in the formulation of a well-formed dowsing question. They are as follows:

1. **Avoid ambiguous words or terms in the question**.

While this might appear to be obvious, it actually requires clear thinking. For example, many new dowsers, upon being told of the importance of good question will use a word like 'good' in a question. Now, such a term might appear to have meaning in the context of the question, but closer examination will reveal that the word 'good' can have a wide variety of meanings and interpretations. 'Good' can apply to physical health, mental, emotional or spiritual health or be a term relative to some other person, place or thing. Without stating explicitly what the 'good' is concerned with, it is possible that the question will be badly formed and the resultant answer, while appearing to be useful is, in fact, useless because of the use of such a vague term. Any word, like 'good', which is comparative, needs to be explained in the question what is being compared with what, and to what degree.

A brief moment of reflection will expose the weakness in words like 'should' (moral imperative provided by whom based on what?) or 'better' (compared to what and to what degree?) or any comparative term at all. (Comparatives include: harder, hardest, quicker, quickest, faster, fastest, richer, poorer, worse, better, more/most complete, happier, happiest, easier, easiest, simpler, simplest, safer, safest, and most/least helpful. A quick search online will help you see whether your question contains a comparative and, if so, whether it is appropriate to do so.)

2. **Have a goal in mind.**

That is, have a reason for asking the question. Without some clear goal in mind, the likelihood is that the question will be woolly or vague in some fashion. There should be a purpose in mind which is obvious to the dowser. A water dowser asks to find water; that's the goal. It is actionable and makes sense. However, if the goal is to satisfy some idle curiosity about some person from whom no permission (q.v.) has been granted, then the resulting question lacks focus, lacks a clear goal. Without that, the intention is much weaker and the result will be of far less use (and probably far less accurate).

3. **Include all the relevant aspects of any situation pertaining to the object of the inquiry, including those you take for granted.**

It is easiest to think of this rule as being the application of six principal aspects. If each of the following are accounted for in the question, and given that there is no ambiguity, then it is reasonable to assume that the question would be well-formed.

The six aspects are those which are taught to all journalists who cover a story. In this instance, their story must cover or account for **Who**, **What**, **Where**, **Why**, **How** and **When**.

4. **The answer to the question can be either Yes or No and nothing else.**

Although dowsing answers are binary (yes/no - see BINARY NATURE OF DOWSING), there are times when it can seem that they do not meet that criteria. For example, a very common answer is found by using a scale (see SCALES) or list of either -10 to +10 or 0 to 100 or something similar. In this case, it might, to a non-dowser, look like that is not a simple yes/no answer. However, it really is, because the place on the scale of the answer will correspond to a 'yes' and all other points on the scale (for the question being asked) will be 'no'. The trick for beginning dowsers is not to get so involved in making the question that they overlook the fact that they are really wanting a single answer and not leave it open-ended.

If your question can be easily seen to include these factors, you are well on your way to becoming better at dowsing. But, as stated, often the obvious is overlooked in one way or another and, in the haste to begin dowsing, a question is formulated which lacks some significant part, making the whole structure weak.

For example, let us suppose that the object of the inquiry is to determine whether or not a particular bottle of mineral supplements is worth purchasing.

What is the goal of the purchase? Let us assume it is to help you improve the state of your nails, making them stronger than they presently are.

How will that goal be measured? Assume that you take the pills as stated, then it would be safe to assume that, by the end of the month there should be some noticeable difference. In this case, your nails should be significantly stronger, less liable to breaking and should be thicker than when you started.

Now that there is a definite, measurable goal, the question can begin to be formulated;

"On a scale of 1 to 10, with 10 being the best and strongest nails I can achieve in one month, what does this bottle of minerals dowse as, for me, if taken as directed over the coming month?"

Note the various aspects of the above question:

"On a scale of 1 to 10..." is the yes/no part. There will be an answer given here.

"...With 10 being the best and strongest nails I can achieve in one month..." This is the goal. It is measurable (to the person involved, they know the state of their own nails) and has a time period. This covers the 'who' aspect and the 'when' aspect, also the 'what' aspect.

"....if taken as directed over the coming months?" This is the 'how'. The 'where' is confined to where the pills would be taken (presumably before meals) and is part of the 'how' in this case.

The 'why' aspect is to gain stronger nails and is an inherent part of the goal-setting.

This question is much better than asking something like, "Will these tablets help my nails get stronger?" It is to be hoped that the difference between the two is quite evident.

R

Radiesthesia

The idea basic to radiesthesia is that the shape of the pendulum or its composition gives it special properties. This is more popular as a concept in France and throughout Europe and far less so in the United Kingdom and America.

The term was coined by a Catholic priest, Abbé Alexis Bouly, after World War One. It was derived from the Latin for radiation and the Greek for perception and entered the English language in the 1930's. The original usage of Bouly and his later compatriots was in dowsing to investigate and understand the non-visual radiations (as they perceived them to be) emanating from all things; human, animal and mineral.

Although many dictionaries will define radiesthesia as being the same as dowsing, the emphasis on shapes and their importance as well as radiations from bodies, as well as in the 'reading' of energy levels, has tended to make this one type of dowsing, distinct from the general use and application of the skill. Some followers will speak of dowsing as being confined to the finding of water and all else as being radiesthesia.

Like most apparent divisions within dowsing (See e.g. BOVIS, LONG PENDULUM, UNIVERSAL PENDULUM) it appears to be more of a mental way of constructing a paradigm about dowsing which can be applied as a sort of formula or similar to help the dowser fit his or her world view into the results obtained. As with most such mental constructs, the results and efficacy vary from dowser to dowser, and do not necessarily strictly follow the original paradigm, but shift slightly from person to person.

Radiesthesia, then, is one such construct which speaks of dowsing as sensing the various emanations which can be dowsed and also, in the European tradition, of pendulums which can themselves radiate certain supposed wave forms or energies.

There is very little to distinguish between proponents of radiesthesia and 'ordinary' dowsing, in terms of results. The main difference lies in the belief that the pendulums themselves (of various styles and designs and materials) are considered to be an important and indeed vital part of healing and other energy techniques. (See also PENDULUM HEALING, NEGATIVE GREEN, FUNDAMENTAL BEAMS and RAYS OF UNION)

Radionics

Radionics has sometimes been called dowsing but with no real justification. According to the British Radionic Association, "Radionics is a healing technique in which our natural intuitive faculties are used both to discover the energetic disturbances underlying illness and to encourage the return of a normal energetic field that supports health. It is independent of the distance between practitioner and patient. Radionics can be used to help humans and animals and in agriculture."

They go on to say that "disciplined dowsing" is basic to a radionics practice. However, as it is stated quite clearly that it is a healing modality, it is not the same as dowsing. Radionics is based on the assumption that every living body emits some type of electromagnetic radiation, energy or similar and that the detection of such can permit diagnosis and that a similar radiation can be transmitted to bring about treatment at a distance.

It really originated with Dr Albert Abrams (1863 - 1924) who proposed that electronic radiations were at the root of all matter and that when electrons were vibrating wrongly, disease resulted.

A radionics machine can be quite complicated to look at. Some of them have circuitry inside, others have none. The only approximation to dowsing occurs in the setting of the dials (the frequency) which is often accomplished by turning each of the dials in turn whilst rubbing a finger on a small 'stick pad' and setting the dial at whatever position it is at when the finger no longer moves easily (i.e., it sticks at that point). That is comparable to dowsing which position or number the dials should be at. Beyond that, however, the rest of the treatment sequences and the ideology behind them have nothing more to do with dowsing.

∾

RAYS OF UNION

Rays of union is one explanation for how the dowser homes in on the target. It seems to have become most popular in or around the 1930's.

The explanation runs somewhat in the following fashion:

Objects which are the same have rays connecting them. So, for example, a key is connected by rays of similarity to all other keys. Therefore, if the dowser is searching for an object, such as a lost gold ring, then by holding a similar object in the hand as a 'witness' (q.v.), it is supposed that the search is made easier because of the ray of union which is said to exist between the two objects.

Another use of the term is that, if a stone or similar object on a line of energy is moved for one reason or another, it still is connected to the line of energy by a ray of union.

It used to be that the first explanation was quite popular but has since become less so.

The idea itself is open to easy criticism as follows. The idea of similarity is, surely, open to the dowser at the time of dowsing. What degree of similarity is necessary for the witness to be of use is, likewise, open to interpretation. For example, if the search is for a cake, and the dowser holds a witness in the form of a cup cake (when the target is a birthday sponge cake) and becomes tired and eats the cup cake, at what point does the ray of union no longer hold? Or is it the fact that it is inside the dowser which still counts? In which case is all consumed food able to form a ray of union with all other food?

The philosophical oddities of this concept serve, at least, to be intellectually interesting, if not wholly convincing from a practical point of view. The point being, one supposes, is that if a belief (q.v.) is strong enough, then it matters little to anyone else except the dowser as to how such a thing might work.

As an aside, the 'similarity' aspect of rays of union is an echo of the philosopher Plato's concept of universal forms, and the interested reader is encouraged to pursue this avenue and see how this might be made to correlate more closely (or not) with the idea of rays of union.

~

REICHENBACH

Baron Karl von Reichenbach, although not directly concerned with investigating or explaining dowsing, nevertheless proposed a theory to partly explain pendulum dowsing.

For various reasons, Reichenbach believed in what he termed the 'Odic' force (q.v.), which was emitted from all objects, animate and inanimate. Some few 'sensitives' as he termed them, were able to see such emissions, or auras. However, the vast majority of people were not sufficiently sensitive and for them, the only method of detecting 'od' (as he termed the Odic force) was via a pendulum.

The concept of some sort sort of invisible force at work in the universe, detectable in various ways by sensitive persons, has given rise to a whole subset of dowsing inquiry involving charts, scales and rates. (See e.g.

BOVIS SCALE, LONG PENDULUM, SIDEREAL PENDULUM, and
THEORY OF RATES)

~

Religion & Dowsing

There are and always have been two diametrically opposed schools of
thought where religion has met with dowsing. Although both schools still
exist, that of the religious opposition to dowsing is the predominant one
today.

Many religious leaders have taken and continue to take a view that
dowsing is, in some ways, the work of the devil or evidence that the
dowsing reaction shows that, somehow, the dowser is in league with or
under the influence of some irreligious or downright evil aspect. This has
been a constant thread throughout the history of dowsing.

In a way, it makes perfect sense because when a dowser's tool moves
without any apparent muscular activity to initiate it, then some invisible
and hitherto unexplained force must be the cause. In earlier times, the
obvious explanation available was that such movement was the result of
devils or imps or other such non-godly creatures.

The argument was that if the movement could not be explained by
recourse to God or the angels, which was not seen as being likely, then the
natural stance to take was that it was not anything heavenly or godly
which caused such un-natural movement. That it was due to devils or
imps was implied by the fact that water or minerals were revealed by no
obvious human ability. If it was a human ability, all humans would be able
to do it, ergo it was non-human, therefore, non-godly and so must be
caused by devils or imps.

Martin Luther, originator of Protestantism, declared in 1518 that dowsing
for metals went against the first commandment. Gaspar Schott, a Jesuit, in
1662 declared that dowsing was superstitious or satanic, although he
wasn't sure that the devil always moved the rod.

Despite some dowsers' claims that the church, particularly the Catholic church, supports dowsing, a quick survey of Catholic forums online makes it clear that, either the participants know very little of it beyond dowsing for water, or they talk of it as divination (q.v.), which is expressly forbidden. In most cases, the current religious attitude toward dowsing is highly dubious and very much concerned with it being against current teaching.

Such an attitude is hardly surprising when many dowsers refer to isolated verses in the Bible which supposedly support the idea of dowsing (See HISTORY OF DOWSING). Taking such references, which are of dubious value anyway, and using them to support a belief, is hardly likely to encourage practicing Christians to accept the validity of dowsing. It seems to be more of an effort to persuade the fence-sitters that dowsing has a long, valid and chronicled history, when no such thing exists and it is not necessary to adopt this approach anyway. If the sole purpose of such references is to show dowsing in a congenial light, it is a far better approach to simply show the value of dowsing in everyday life, rather than rely on dubious references to such things as Moses' rod, or striking rocks with rods or some such passage which are only clear to the person quoting them.

Having said that, there has been a long and very fruitful association of religion with dowsing. The Jesuits, long-time intellectual arm of Catholicism, despite such members as Schott, were the first people to make serious study of, and suggest theories about, dowsing.

In fact, Catholics have provided much of the emphasis in the exploration and understanding of dowsing. For example, the Jesuit, Father Kircher, one of the first proponents of experimental science, in 1650, showed that the movement came from the person holding the tool.

In 1701, the Holy Inquisition passed a decree banning the use of dowsing or divining rods in criminal trials. That there had to be an official decree on the subject suggests that there were sufficient uses of dowsing to require it and that, prior to it, the Inquisition was not automatically averse to its use. The most well-documented example of the use of dowsing in a criminal aspect is that of the dowser Aymar (q.v.). The controversy raised by

Aymar's actions led to the denunciation of dowsing by a well-known Cistercian (Armand Jean le Bouthillier de Rancé (Abbé de la Trappe)), and also by Abbé Pirot, the chancellor of the University of Paris. Both such attempts, and all such later attempts, were doomed from the beginning as dowsing was investigated and used by clerics with apparent impunity.

Another clergyman, the Bishop of Grenoble, working with one of the best documented water dowsers, Bléton (q.v.), in the eighteenth century, discovered a rule, now known as the Bishop's Rule (q.v.), for finding the depth of a water vein.

Abbé Mermet (q.v.) (1866 - 1937), was the first notable dowser to use a pendulum to assist in medical diagnosis. Indeed the French Catholic influence on the development of dowsing is one of the most notable ways in which religion has supported the skill.

It is not the intention to scour all possible religious references to act as supporting dowsing. There is enough of that readily available to the casual researcher. What is important is that the religious views on dowsing, whilst they might appear to be condemnatory in nature, nevertheless show that, over a long period of time, amounting to centuries, while some clergymen have been denouncing dowsing, others, at the same time, have been actively investigating it and moving it forward.

Many dowsers wish to claim religious attitudes as supportive of dowsing for the social proof it offers. Many religious people wish to denounce dowsing as going against religious teaching. It is highly likely that any possible resolution to this lies somewhere in between the two extremes.

Until then, those who wish to see dowsing as the work of the devil in various forms, and those who see the church as broadly supportive will continue to try to prove the other wrong. It is not a fight which can be won by either side. Also, it is not a fight worth fighting, as the end result will achieve very little when all is said and done.

∼

REMOTE DOWSING

Remote dowsing is where the dowser is not able to be in the same physical location as the target. (See ON-SITE DOWSING)

For example, being unable to enter a field for whatever reason, the dowser would be able to locate a target using triangulation (see MAP DOWSING).

However, most remote dowsing takes place usually at some considerable distance from the target. So, for example, a dowser might use remote dowsing to locate a missing object on a property the other side of the world.

The use of remote dowsing, together with examples of success in such areas, has given rise to various theories (q.v.) of dowsing to explain this ability.

∽

Rhabdomancy

This is the term for divination through rods or wands or sticks. You will find that several dictionaries define this term as the use of dowsing with rods or wands and will give the origin of the word as somewhere in the early 1600's. However, the classical definition is that of divination using these instruments. The efficacy of such divination was supposed to depend on the ceremonies and Kabbalistic words which accompanied its use. This has nothing to do with dowsing.

(See DIVINATION)

S

Scales

Scales are very useful. They can add a depth and refinement to the usual 'Yes' or 'No' response. A scale can consist of any particular range, or can be constructed to consist of whatever the dowser requires. The basic premise of scales used in dowsing is that they have to have a definite gradation to them; numbers or percentages, low to high, for example. The usual scales consist of numbers, but there is no reason why they could not use color, distance or any other gradation which is useful to the dowser.

For example, a scale of percentage could be used to indicate the strength of an answer. Therefore, instead of a simple 'Yes', the percentage scale could be used to indicate the *amount* of 'Yes.' A very low percentage would indicate a very weak 'Yes.' Such a thing would be of use when trying to decide between two or more possible answers, both of them being positive, as when testing for which supplement of three would most closely meet the goals of the question (q.v.).

Instead of a percentage, the scale could run from 1 to 10 instead.

Of course, the extension of the scale into negative numbers is perfectly permissible, as the strength of the 'No' response could then be tested as well. Therefore, scales can be constructed (or found online) running from -100% to +100% and from -10 to +10. Which is used is, of course, down to personal preference.

In a sense the Mager Rosette (q.v.) is a type of scale, but it uses color to differentiate between possible answers.

The Bovis scale (q.v.) was based originally on the Ångström to assess levels of vitality (amongst other things).

Whereas charts (q.v.) are used to select more easily from a range of possible answers, scales are generally used to refine a particular answer.

A scale can be linear or arranged in a circle or semi-circle, depending on the whim of the dowser. No one arrangement is better than any other, except for ease of use for the individual.

(See also THEORY OF RATES)

~

Science & Dowsing

It is not the purpose of this encyclopedia to document or dissect the various scientific examinations of dowsing which have occurred. These are easily assessed by the reader through a cursory examination of such attempts using the internet, as well as by perusing Christopher Bird's *The Divining Hand*. What is of interest, however, is the relationship between the two subjects, as that will tend to color any examination or interpretation.

Science and dowsing are not, at the time of writing, comfortable companions. Science tends to see dowsing as inhabiting the outer fringes of the 'real' or physical world. And, as such, it has little to offer (to the scientists, at any rate) which could enhance scientific understanding.

It is true that there have been a few scientists who have bothered to look at the subject with anything other than scorn. Some have sought to explain it by introducing new ideas, such as the 'dowson' particle (proposed by Professor Vincent Reddish). Others have sought to identify whereabouts in the body any particular activity or response might be happening. This is usually carried out by selectively shielding different areas until the dowser no longer responds.

But these are a long way from being able to offer a coherent theory as to how dowsing might work. (See THEORIES)

Dowsers, on the one hand, are interested in having scientists examine the subject because such interest would, they argue, make dowsing more popular and more mainstream. They often bewail the fact that science and scientists do not take them and what they do seriously.

However, until it can be shown that a serious investigation of dowsing would probably reveal information or data which could have broad application elsewhere, then it remains unlikely that science will take a long, hard look at the subject.

It should be pointed out that people do not rush to a new idea because of the science behind it. They rush because it will solve a problem they have, make them feel better about themselves or it serves a need they already have. Those are the only reasons which are behind any innovation, not the science.

Dowsers, of course, rarely help their cause by being unable to agree on the fundamentals of dowsing. Strange origins for the answers, theories of unseen guides or helpers, reliance on other invisible aspects of the world, such as auras and chakras and the catch-all term, 'energy;' all such things serve to push the scientific community further away. A scientist who chooses to investigate dowsing as it presently stands would probably be an independent researcher looking at the subject as a sideline, or a particularly thick-skinned person who, for whatever reasons, is able to ignore the stern condemnation of his peers.

At one time or another, there is bound to be a turning point, when dowsing is looked at more carefully and sympathetically. However, it would be wise not to expect the floodgates to open wide and for dowsing to be welcomed with open arms into the realm of science. It may take many years from that initial breakthrough before dowsing gains any wider credibility among scientists.

The main reason dowsing wants scientific recognition is because science is seen as being an approach to understanding or apprehending the truth (q.v.) of whatever is the subject of scientific investigation. This, of course, assumes that such a monolithic thing as 'the truth' does actually exist and that we are capable of knowing it to be so. Neither of which are, in themselves, necessarily true.

The other problem facing dowsing, in terms of scientific investigation, is that when a dowser dowses, using a tool (or not) it is the dowser who is both the observer of any experiments and the subject of them. It is not the tool which does the work, but the dowser. Therefore, any scientific investigation which seeks to separate one from the other is, by definition, not then investigating dowsing. And to try and devise an experiment which adheres to current good scientific practice and also accepts the duality of the dowsing phenomenon is going to be very difficult indeed.

Finally, it is important to point out that, because of the subject / object paradox, it is not in the least surprising that many dowsers involved in research of one kind or another find that they have an idea or a response which gets them to thinking, and then they begin to get exactly the results they think should exist. There are many such examples through the history of this subject. Such an approach naturally does little to help a 'scientific' acceptance of the subject even if that is exactly how the world works.

~

SENSITIVITY

Sensitivity to external influences is an area which is occasionally suggested as an being capable of explaining how dowsing works. (See HYPERSENSITIVITY)

But there might also be reason to suspect that sensitivity outside of the five senses might also prove of interest in helping to explain not just dowsing but also other aspects of human actions and reactions.

Numerous experiments over many years have shown time and again that the human body, indeed *all* living bodies are remarkably susceptible to very small influences. These influences include, but are not limited to, electrical energy at extremely low levels, such things as focused thoughts (intentions) as well as times of day and phases of the moon. Such sensitivity may well have a varying effect on the dowser as he or she works, according to the individual sensitivity and the particular target under investigation. It is an area worthy of more research as it could help dowsers discover optimal dowsing conditions, if such exists.

Most of these responses within the human body are at a subliminal level. Nevertheless, they are identifiable as such and it may prove that some, or all, such sensitivities are somehow feeding into the dowsing response.

Although there is a real lack of serious investigation into such areas as they relate to dowsing, it is reasonable to assume that any one hypothesis presently asserted as being true is, in all likelihood, to be wide of the mark.

Many people want to explain how dowsing works. Ideas have been proposed and discarded over centuries with no real conclusion being made (See THEORIES). To assume that the sensitivity of the human body (or mind) is solely responsible for how dowsing works is to ignore the vast chasm which then opens up demanding explanation of precisely *which* sensitivity (or sensitivities) is responsible and exactly how that might work.

As we have not yet gained sufficient understanding of the subconscious (q.v.) to allow for definitive statements of its functions, resources and abilities to be agreed upon, to assert that sensitivity alone is responsible is not a helpful position to adopt either.

∼

Seven Levels Of Dowsing

The idea of seven levels of dowsing ability appears to have originated with Terry Ross (died 2000, one-time President of the American Society of Dowsers) and given wider airing by one of his students, Sig Lonegren, himself a past Vice-President of both the American and British Societies of Dowsing.

Although there are some serious issues with this system, and those will be examined later on, the various levels are as follows:

Level One is where the dowsing takes place over the target. This would be, for example, on-site dowsing (q.v.).

Level Two is where the dowser is not directly over the target but the target is still within sight. For example, standing on the edge of a field and dowsing whereabouts in the field the target is (i.e., direction of flow of underground water, the location of a septic tank etc.).

Level Three is dowsing where the target is not in sight. This would be remote dowsing (q.v.). A typical example of this would be map dowsing (q.v.).

Level Four is deviceless dowsing (q.v.), where the answer is sensed in some fashion by the dowser without the use of tools.

Level Five is where energy (q.v.) is channeled to alter things. So, for example, a Level Three dowser might be able to sense some health issues, a level Five dowser would be able to remediate those issues.

Level Six is a step up from the previous level in that, instead of channeling energy to heal, the health issue (for example) is made to disappear. So, instead of having cancer, the X-ray after a Level Six dowser had worked on it, would be clean and clear.

Level Seven was not easily explained, being along the lines of the Creator and the dowser are as one, although what that means specifically is not clear. It is, apparently, the highest level you can operate on and still have a physical existence.

The objections to this classification system are as follows. Firstly, the idea that there are various levels of dowsing ability is, in and of itself, dubious. Although, at first glance, a scale of dowsing ability does have an appeal, it is not something which is justified when one considers the various levels of expertise shown by people when they come to dowsing. If you consider that different people will be able to dowse effectively over a target or via map-dowsing, it does not mean that they are operating at different levels. It is just as valid to say that, for them, the way they obtain the results (remotely or on-site) means only that that is the best way dowsing works for them at that time. Some people will take to map-dowsing quickly and struggle with on-site dowsing, and vice versa.

Secondly, levels five, six and seven seem to move progressively away from dowsing to intention and to spirituality. These levels appear to be somewhat arbitrary and serve more to elevate dowsing (in dowsers' eyes at least) into something wonderfully esoteric.

It is not a dowsing ability to heal. It never has been considered as such in the past. Healers healed, dowsers dowsed. To arrogate such abilities and claim them for dowsing seems disingenuous to say the least. The last three levels could, quite easily, find a place in a modern book on energetic healing and have no reference to dowsing whatsoever and still be perfectly understandable and acceptable. Level seven, in particular, is more to do with spiritual enlightenment than dowsing. Whilst it is perfectly proper and acceptable to state that, through the use of dowsing in helping to understand oneself one can become more spiritually attuned, it is not acceptable to say that spiritual enlightenment is the direct result of dowsing ability.

And that, surely, must be the test by which such claims for dowsing should be judged. Is it a claim which demands the specific skill of dowsing to justify it or can it be understood without reference to dowsing at all? In this case, the last three levels can be understood in their own right without regard to dowsing or the ability to dowse and should therefore be safely ignored as having nothing to do with dowsing at all.

∿

Sidereal Pendulum

The Sidereal or Sideric Pendulum is a name give to a pendulum (q.v.) which appeared to be popular around the beginning of the twentieth century. The word 'sideric' is archaic and means 'pertaining to iron'. However, the references made to such a pendulum speak of using a gold ring, not an iron one. This would suggest that 'sideric' is a misnomer. The word 'sidereal', on the other hand usually refers to a measure of time, based upon distant stars, such as the sidereal year. In this case, however, from descriptions of its use, it would appear that a more useful definition would seem to be based on the concept of measurement by stars in that it is based on revolutions. One assumes that the concept of 'as above, so below' is behind this somewhere. Therefore, this would seem to be a clumsy term for a simple pendulum which was used to ascertain information by discerning the movements it made.

It might be claimed, therefore, that a Foucault pendulum could also be considered as a sidereal pendulum in that it shows the change in movement of large pendulum over time caused by the rotation of the Earth. Such a pendulum, however, has nothing to do with dowsing. (A Foucault pendulum is named after the French physicist of the 19th Century and was used as a simple demonstration of the rotation of the Earth by suspending a heavy weight from a very long wire (somewhere between 40 and 90 feet). The time taken for a complete rotation of such a pendulum is one sidereal day.)

A picture purporting to show a sidereal pendulum (https://yooniqimages.com/images/detail/102109847/with-the-sideric-pendulum-you-can-learn-the-future-and-do-all-sorts-of-other-amazing-things, accessed August 2015) appears to be showing a pendulum suspended over the alphabet, similar to a ouija board. Another picture shown on http://www.oocities.org/odinistlibrary/OLArticles/Articles/karlspiesberger.htm, accessed August 2015, also shows a pendulum over a set of runes.

The more likely explanation of the term dates back to the early 19th Century and the introduction of the concept of invisible universal forces which were able to act upon pendulums. (See THEORY OF RATES)

However, there is an interesting article by Sir Arthur Conan Doyle introducing this pendulum. In this article ("The Sideric Pendulum" published in *The Strand Magazine* in August 1920), he begins by saying it is, to the Spiritualists, a well-known method of communication. He says that the movement of the pendulum over gold and amber (which he claims are male, without explanation) will be circular, and that over silver it is oval (oval being the female reaction), whilst steel and bronze are longitudinal.

He calls the left to right motion, the 'evil reaction,' and claims to find it over alcohol.

In responding to criticism of the article, Conan Doyle describes the sideric pendulum in the following fashion (published in the *Otago Daily Times,* 21 December 1920):

"Take a piece of fine string or silk, tie one end round the finger, and attach a weight — a gold ring for choice — to the other end. Stand north and south. Now hold the ring about an inch above any photograph. Within a minute the ring, if the photograph is of a male, will describe circles; if it is of a female it will describe an ellipse."

Note the reference to a specific orientation of the body and the inference that the pendulum is held still until movement is made apparent.

A Czech website (http://detektorweb.cz , accessed August 2015) also shows an undated advertisement for a sex detector (the sideric pendulum) which is called 'A Wonderful Fun Maker, A Scientific Instrument, Better Than The Ouija Board' and says that you can 'Instantly detect the sex of humans, animals or insects'. The accompanying diagrams show that, according to the sales people, a circular motion indicates a female and forward and backward movement indicates a male. Different to Conan Doyle's observations, you will notice, which again illustrates the importance of the individual dowser knowing his or her own responses.

As an aside on this issue, it is interesting to note that pendulums and dowsing became much more intertwined in the 1920's. In that period, when it was gaining more converts, pendulums were referred to by a range of exotic names such as Ayada-Woholo, Sex Detector, Sex Indicator, Cyko-Sphere, Sideric Mystery or Chevreul's Pendulum. The latter term was after the French investigator of dowsing, a highly regarded chemist who studied the pendulum and its use in dowsing in the 1880's. (Thanks to http://theinnereye.tumblr.com/page/2, accessed August 2015)

The term is still somewhat alive. A book called *Reveal the power of the pendulum : secrets of the sidereal pendulum : a complete survey of pendulum dowsing* was published by Foulsham in 1987.

~

SKEPTICISM

Skepticism is an excellent state of mind, a useful analytical tool when applied openly and with reasoning. At its best, it is a questioning attitude to knowledge, facts or opinions stated as facts. At its worst, however, it is used to deny any knowledge, fact or opinion stated as fact without question which contradicts the skeptic's beliefs. This is the general attitude when it comes to dowsing; it is more similar to an unreasoning antipathy. And then the term is used as a shield behind which this passion to debunk, instead of to examine and analyze, is then thought to have disproved dowsing on all grounds.

It is water dowsing which is most usually attacked. Other types of dowsing are considered to be so far away from the present scientific status quo as to not be worth wasting any time at all in debunking. The skeptics' arguments are usually along the lines of 'the dowsers are fooling both themselves and any gullible clients they may acquire', and that 'any apparent success is due solely to luck'. The arguments need not be examined in any great detail, as they bear a sad similarity in that they expose an unwillingness to actually make a detailed analysis of the phenomenon. Instead, they usually base their assumptions or convictions on one or two personal cases or on some populist debunking which also lacks any scientific rigor.

Any skeptic who is true to what skepticism really is about should be ready to be swayed by any anomaly into thinking that there is some justification for at least investigating it further. As Carl Sagan noted, "The truth may be puzzling. It may take some work to grapple with. It may be counterintuitive. It may contradict deeply held prejudices. It may not be consonant with what we desperately want to be true. But our preferences do not determine what's true."

His view is an echo of an earlier 17th Century scientist, Robert Boyle (of Boyle's Law), who experimented with dowsing but was unable to have any success. He acknowledged, however, that others could succeed. He said, "I must content myself to say what I am wont to do when my opinion is asked of those things which I dare not peremptorily reject, and yet am not convinced of: namely, that they that have seen them can much more reasonably believe them than they that have not."

It is not the intention here to state that any skeptic is automatically a scoundrel, nor every dowser a saint. Yet the problem with denying the truth of water dowsing specifically is that it overlooks the anomalies in its practice over centuries. There have been many instances where the location of water cannot be explained by traditional (i.e. scientific) means.

There have been some few investigations of water dowsing. However, these have been typified by placing the dowser in an unnatural setting, seeking to find the success rate in detecting whether water is flowing in a hidden pipe or not. Naturally, the success or not is usually computed statistically, which is not how dowsing is actually determined in the field. The failure of any distinct departure from the norm is usually cited as reason to dismiss the whole field completely.

Yet, the anomalies remain and it is the existence of these, which cannot be taken as pure luck when every other possibility has been accounted for, which demand at least some investigation.

It is not the intention of this article to collect, collate and display such anomalies. However, it *is* the intention here to make it clear that skepticism is a valuable analytical tool which has been used too infrequently in dowsing to entitle its supporters to deserve respect.

For those who would care to discover some of the anomalies for themselves, they would be well advised to study Professor William Barrett's detailed investigation of water dowsing, published under the title *The Credibility Of Dowsing*.

One of the main ways in which skeptics and dowsers meet and interact is because of the dowser's wish to persuade non-dowsers of dowsing's wonderful nature. The excitement which dowsing can provide to new dowsers can lead them to attempt to pass on their excitement to others by demonstrating this new-found skill. It nearly always ends in disappointment for the dowser and changes nothing at all.

The desire to want others to experience dowsing for themselves and thus to take it seriously is, of course, perfectly understandable. However, changing a firmly held opinion is rarely going to be accomplished in five or ten minutes. Skeptics need to arrive at a state of doubt first, then perhaps moving on to one of acceptance. But if doubt is all that can be achieved, then that is good enough.

One final note about skepticism is that it would appear that those who are skeptical of dowsing can often, through their presence, adversely affect a dowser's results. It is not always true, but there are plenty of anecdotal cases which would seem to verify this. Therefore, as a new dowser, it would be prudent to stay away from skeptics until a degree of confidence is gained. Why this occurs is hard to say, but, if there is any truth to the idea that emotions or attitudes can be both broadcast and received, then it would seem to suggest that it is the more strong-minded and self-confident dowsers who would perform best under skeptic scrutiny. This appears to be borne out by the facts of cases which have been investigated carefully. Again, refer to *The Credibility of Dowsing* for many such instances.

~

SPACE CLEARING

Space clearing is the term given to energetic balancing or removal of 'negative' energies (see ENERGY) in an environment (See also BAUBIOLOGIE).

Relating it to dowsing, it became a more widely known application of this skill after von Pohl (q.v.) investigated Vilsbiburg (q.v.). Since that time, dowsing has proven highly effective at identifying so called 'noxious zones' or areas which are unhealthy for the inhabitants.

The actual space clearing is not achieved by dowsing in any form at all. Dowsing is, instead, used to identify those areas which need attention and it can also be used to ascertain which process or method wold be most effective in ameliorating the situation.

Both the identification of such areas as well as the effect of them upon humans are indications of the sensitivity (q.v.) of the human organism at work.

There are many theories about what causes the issues in environments, but it is true to say that the effects of such places on health has been noted over centuries.

What the reader should be aware of, however, is that dowsing is only the method of locating and identifying such places. It is not, in any way, involved in their remediation. Those who say that their pendulum cleared the room, for example, are guilty of sloppy thinking or of confusing dowsing with intention (q.v.).

~

Spanish Needles

Of all the various dowsing tools (q.v.), Spanish Needles probably rank as the strangest in idea as well as being unique in that it takes two people to use them.

The origin of these needles is unclear, although there seems to be an (unsubstantiated) idea that they were used in the mid 16th Century in America, having been described in a 1569 publication. That they were called Spanish needles was due, it appears, to their use by Spaniards at that time as they were searching for gold. Another term for them is 'dipping needles', from the action they have. (They are also sometimes referred to as Mexican Needles - presumably because they were also used in that area of the world.)

Most of the reports about them concern their use for finding gold, which was certainly one of the driving forces behind Spanish exploration in the south and west of the U.S.. And it was also said in the 1569 book (*Natural Magic*, by Giambatista della Porta) that they were supposed to be particularly useful in revealing treasure.

Sometimes there appears to be confusion when referring to them as Spanish Magnets or Miner's Compass. A compass will certainly decline over a large mass of iron, and some placer gold is found near black sands, which has a high iron content. It is therefore not too much of a stretch in imagination to conclude that compasses were certainly used by gold hunters in western America. Maybe, from that association, the name 'Spanish' was added, but that is not how the true Spanish Needles operate.

As noted previously, this is a tool for two people to use simultaneously. It is possible, though by no means mandatory, that a man and a woman was the ideal combination, allowing for the supposed benefit of having both sexes working together.

The four rods, one for each hand, are generally quite short, being no longer than six inches, although the precise length would be a matter of personal preference. At one end of each rod there is a nick, or indentation, forming a small depression or a fork. In operation these ends are interlocked as the two operators face each other.

The rods will, supposedly, point at the target (also, presumably treasure of some kind). The two dowsers then move in unison until the rods make another movement, and so on until the target is located, presumably by a dipping motion, hence the alternate name.

Obviously, it will require a good degree of cooperation and understanding before anything useful can be achieved with these tools.

It is probably safe to say that any such operation of these 'needles' would be to find some commonly agreed upon and obvious target, such as deliberately buried gold or placer gold. They were used simply to point out the location but not also used to indicate depth.

Of course, the real interest in these tools is the question as to why they were developed in the first place? Was it because two prospectors did not trust each other and wanted something which they could both use simultaneously, or was there a different, less confrontational origin to them?

We shall probably never know and they shall remain as one of the oddities in dowsing.

STANDING Stones

Standing stones or menhirs have frequently been attractive to dowsers usually because the dowsers wish to investigate either the history of the place or the energy (q.v.) of the stone itself.

Standing stones, because of their antiquity, have long proved of interest. They are large and they have been in place for probably thousands of years and so act as a direct, physical and visual link with our ancestors in some fashion. It is no wonder then that they still are the center of investigation.

However, with regard to dowsing, they have been the cause of various ideas or theories, but without any real consensus beyond the basic agreement that there is usually some form of dowseable energy emanating from them.

The precise nature of that energy as well as what that energy is supposed to do or be for is open to debate still.

Standing stones, like stone circles, will always attract ideas as to their purpose, history or nature.

A detailed study of them is not appropriate here. Interested readers should look to earth energy investigations as well as esoteric explanations of places such as Avebury, Stonehenge, Callanish and the like.

~

Stone Circles

See STANDING STONES

~

STRIKING

One term, common to both oil and water, is that of 'striking'. The dowser (and driller) 'strike' oil and water. The reason for the use of this word might well be because the dowsing tool, usually a rod of some kind when used on-site, moves downwards, or appears to 'strike' down. One of the early terms for a dowsing rod was the 'striking rod.' So, it possible that this old term came to be applied to the discovery, rather than the implement.

❧

Subconscious, The

The role of the subconscious in everyday life is still largely unexplained. With regard to dowsing, however, we can limit ourselves to just looking at three areas.

First is the effect that beliefs hidden in the subconscious might have on your dowsing effectiveness and accuracy. (See BELIEFS for a more detailed explanation.)

Secondly, the amount of information stored in the subconscious is unknown, but seems to be very large. As such, there is the possibility that there are influences at work, other than beliefs, which could impinge in some fashion on the dowsing ability (see PAST LIVES).

Thirdly, as the mechanisms at work in the subconscious are largely unknown, the ability to respond to subliminal information when dowsing might occur there. The precise nature of the ideomotor effect (q.v.) is also unclear, but there is reason to assume that it takes place in some fashion in the subconscious.

The role of the subconscious (q.v.) in dowsing is, therefore, probably highly important, but the precise method of involvement is still open to investigation and discovery.

It has long been accepted, at least since Freud developed psychoanalysis in the late 19th century, that the subconscious or unconscious part of the mind can and does have a definite role to play in the life of any individual. The problem, however, was and remains that it is not possible to directly access the subconscious in the same way as the conscious mind.

With the conscious mind, it is easy to understand the thoughts and ideas which are part of everyday life. They are there and evident to the least introspection. However, the subconscious elements are not so easily examined. Beliefs, ideas, reactions and things seen or heard but not registered by the conscious mind are all stored in there and have been proven empirically to exist.

The intriguing part of this, for the dowser, is that the subconscious mind can interfere with, and intrude into the act of, dowsing and create various confusions, unless specifically noted and accounted for.

Although this might seem far-fetched, enough studies of dowsers and dowsing (albeit in informal and anecdotal ways) have been made and reported to strongly support this statement. It would be most interesting if a properly researched experiment was to be set up and the results noted. It would, however, require a great deal of background work and possibly psychoanalysis as part of the experiment.

Let us assume, for the purpose of explaining this problem, that a dowser has a hidden, subconscious belief (q.v.) about water. From some upsetting moment in childhood, largely forgotten and never consciously thought about, she has a fear of water. Now, when dowsing about water, that fear is still lurking, and, because water is equated with fear and therefore to be avoided at all costs, her accuracy at locating water is much lower than would be expected.

With a little thought, it becomes apparent that other fears and phobias, affecting many different areas of life, could directly or indirectly alter a dowser's ability. From being able to formulate good questions to actually locating targets, the alert dowser should always be looking within to discover potential blocks or problems.

Of course, the subconscious is not, by definition, available for casual, conscious inspection. But, the skill of dowsing does allow the dowser to actually ask questions about what it contains and how it is affecting conscious life.

In this role, dowsing is probably the most useful tool of all. It does permit direct access to the subconscious and thus to finding out what needs to be changed and how to go about affecting that change.

It is important to note that any dowser who is wanting to improve, to learn and to grow, both as a dowser and as a person, should be strongly encouraged to use dowsing to examine and understand the ongoing effect the subconscious is having in life.

~

Switching

Switching is the usual term applied to the circumstance whereby a dowser's yes and no responses are reversed. 'Yes' becomes shown as 'No' and vice versa.

It appears that there are a variety of possible causes for this situation.

1.The dowser is dehydrated and the fine motor responses are no longer reliable.

2.The dowser is standing in or over an area where there are certain conflicting energetic influences. (See GEOPATHIC STRESS)

3.The target of the dowsing is raising conscious or subconscious fears, causing the correct response to be switched. (See BELIEFS)

In each case, it is possible to address the underlying issue through appropriate measures: re-hydrating, moving, and dealing with the emotional issues around the subject.

Another term which is used when such situations arise is that of 'switching polarity.' (See POLARITY. See also IDEOMOTOR EFFECT)

T

Technique

It is sometimes the case that the term 'techniques' becomes interchangeable for the term 'applications' when applied to dowsing.

If the idea is that there are various ways of dowsing, then those are the techniques. If the idea, however, is of the various ways in which dowsing can be used (and that includes the various tools), those are the applications.

So, dowsing techniques might sound susceptible to investigation, in fact there really is only one technique which can be applied.

The basic technique of dowsing is as follows:

1. Generate a well-formed question (assuming permission (q.v.) is not needed!)

2. Enter the dowsing state (q.v.)

3. Obtain the answer

That, in essence, is what all dowsing is about. However, the last part, that of obtaining the answer, can give rise to various ideas of techniques, but those are really only concerning themselves with the use of the tool. The dowsing technique, as with all techniques, is a process which can be refined and mastered with time and practice. Everything else is either preparation or application.

∿

THEORIES

Although the reason for the movement of the dowsing tool is generally agreed upon, by dowsers at least, (see IDEOMOTOR EFFECT), tracing back as to why the movement originates at all is another matter entirely. Non-dowsers, it should be noted, do not necessarily ascribe automatically to the ideomotor theory. Theories as to what might be happening at the moment of obtaining an answer, the moment of intuition (q.v.), has given rise to many different explanations.

These explanations comprise five different groups:

Group 1 assumes that most dowsers are charlatans and that, particularly in the case of water dowsing, they are actually reading and responding to subtle clues on the surface, such as the color of the soil and vegetation, the types of plants, slope of the land and so on.

Group 2 contains theories which assume that there is some physical effect upon the dowser, such as electro-magnetic (q.v.) or other type of radiation, to which the dowser responds. Magnetism (q.v.) is one of the popular theories in this group. (See also RAYS OF UNION)

Group 3 contains theories which seek to explain the movement by assuming that there is some form of ESP, or other psychic ability. This, of course, unlike the previous two groups, cannot be so easily tested experimentally. Into this group can be added the early attempts at explanations such as demons being behind the movement of the tool.

Group 4 contains theories which rely upon the various strange aspects of quantum physics (See QUANTUM THEORY, HOLOGRAPHIC UNIVERSE) to explain how answers are obtained. These theories are also not prone to easy experimentation.

Group 5 contains the idea that there are some sort of emanations from the target of the dowsing to which the dowser is susceptible. (See FUNDAMENTAL BEAMS)

Experiments have been devised which seem to show that some dowsers are very sensitive to very small electro-magnetic fields and to changes in them as the dowser walks. This could be an explanation for some of the results obtained by dowsers. But there is no conclusive evidence as yet. Similarly, the idea that certain areas of the earth have different qualities which can be located by dowsers is something which has a long history, especially in Europe, but would need further detailed investigation.

Neither of those explanations would suffice for any type of distance dowsing. For that, some sort of psi ability is assumed, but not proven.

In brief, there are any number of theories abounding as to what happens when a dowser dowses, but there is nothing which might in any way be considered as proof positive in support of any one of them.

Another way of looking at dowsing is to posit only three possible mechanisms at work. First, that all objects emit radiation of some kind which the dowser 'picks up on' in some fashion.

Second, the dowser emits some kind of radiation which is then detected when it bounces back from the object.

Third, the dowsing effect is purely mental.

These last three were suggested by the author Colin Wilson (a neighbor of T.C. Lethbridge (see LONG PENDULUM), who introduced him to dowsing). From personal experience and from anecdotal evidence of experienced dowsers, there seems to be sufficient consideration to suggest that the mental aspect of dowsing is what is central to it. Certainly, tools are not necessary as has been repeatedly shown by various dowsers throughout the ages (see e.g. ZAHORIS or BLÉTON). The precise nature of how the mind contributes to dowsing is yet to be revealed.

Most dowsers have their own private theories as to what might be behind the process. Some dowsers also do not seem to be bothered by such considerations and are just happy that it works.

It may be that a new line of inquiry will open up possibilities which will result in greater advances. However, what seems to be certain as of now is that it is unlikely that any one theory of dowsing will suffice to explain all the present, practical, applications of this skill. Perhaps there is no dowsing equivalent of a Grand Unified Theory, but rather a set of theories which will explain the various types of dowsing.

As a footnote to this, the following is an example of a strange theory which was reported in *Canada's Victorian Oil Town* by Christina Burr. *The Sarnia Observer* in 1865, reporting of the Enniskillen Township, spoke of an oil smeller (See OIL DOWSING) there whose technique was described thus:

"The operator proceeds across the fields…and occasionally pauses, standing on one foot…While both feet are on the earth, the theory is that a magic circle is formed, and the same sensation is not felt in the nervous system as when the connection is broken by resting on one foot only. Hence the magnetic sensation is all passed through one limb, and whenever the oil is beneath, the feeling is greater or less in force according to its proximity with the surface, or its extent of volume."

It seems there is no end to possible theories! (See SCIENCE AND DOWSING)

~

THEORY OF RATES

There is not really one single theory of rates, but rather a variety of them which has led to a jumble of confusion in dowsing. The idea of 'rates' generally subsists in the concept that there is one or more invisible force or forces at work in the universe and that these permeate or interact with both animate and inanimate objects to a greater or lesser degree. These forces are often only visible to a small number of specially sensitive persons. The rest of humanity has to use instrumentation to perceive them or simply trust that they exist. Thus the idea of the human aura, not readily visible to all, is an example of a generally invisible force.

This concept became of great interest at around the time of the development of electrical theory and experimentation. Various experimenters, who had come into contact with dowsers or dowsing, began to investigate various theories to explain movements of the pendulum (q.v.) or other devices (See THEORIES).

A range of terms began to be used to help explain this invisible 'something' which had to be the cause of the movement of the dowser's tool. Terms such as electrometry, siderism, odic force (q.v.) and organo-electricity began to be used.

In virtually all of the theories there existed the conviction that there was something happening when a pendulum was held over a test piece which could only be explained by some force which permeated the entire universe and of which we were dimly aware, if at all, except through results such as provided by dowsers.

This is the basis for the term 'siderism,' based as it is on the Latin 'sidus' for star, which assumed that a force of the universe permeated everything, including the human body and the pendulum. Thus there can be no separation of man from his surroundings. (See SIDEREAL PENDULUM)

From these beginnings (which, incidentally, are also the beginnings of an awareness that such an intimate connection can therefore provide answers to any question at all), sprang the idea that the use of a tool such as a pendulum could clearly indicate connections between, and properties of, materials.

It is from this idea that theories of rates has emerged. Intrinsic to it is the concept that there are specific qualities within any substance which can be classified by the movement of the pendulum in particular.

The basic tenet of any such system of rates (See BOVIS SCALE, LONG PENDULUM), is that the classification is purely subjective and entirely dependent upon the dowser. Such classifications cannot be confirmed by any existing physical science as it lacks the necessary instrumentation.

Inherent in this approach is the assumption that the dowser is both skillful enough and of sufficient honesty as to be believable, and further, that such knowledge obtained is of a special kind, available only through immediate apprehension incapable of confirmation. It also implies that whatever scale or reading is dowsed by one person will not, in all likelihood, be the same for another dowser using the same set of materials.

The results of such an approach and set of beliefs has led to such things as the Bovis scale (q.v.), fundamental beams (q.v.), and any number of proposed classifications obtained through dowsing, all of which are taken as being immutable and perfect, when, for the reasons given above, that is highly unlikely to be the case.

It seems to be the case that, whenever a scale has been 'discovered' then the underlying theory is built up in some fashion from existing scientific research to bolster the case for its veracity (See, for example, BOVIS SCALE). It is, perhaps, another example of humanity's tendency to justify and underpin a new belief or assertion by referring to previous knowledge, in much the same way as beliefs (q.v.) can become facts in dowsing theory.

As an aside, it is worth pointing out that the concept of a pendulum being able to react to a substance, idea, or mineral in a certain way without interference from any person (the basis of the sidereal pendulum (q.v.)) could lead one to conflate this idea with radiesthesia (q.v.). However, in the latter case, the main contention is that the shape of the pendulum itself is of primary importance, whereas in the former case, it is the supposed force or forces acting upon the pendulum which are of primary importance.

(See also SCALES)

~

THOUGHTFORMS

A thoughtform is defined as a materialized thought which has taken physical form. In other words, it is something which has its origin in a mental state but which has then developed into something which has physical aspects. While such a thing might seem to be more at home the realms of science-fiction films, the concept does have a long history and is most well developed in the Tibetan culture.

There, the idea of a tulpa is in Tibetan teachings where a well-developed mind can bring a being into existence. Indeed, in a book, *Magic and Mystery in Tibet* by Alexandra David-Néel (1929), she wrote that, "…Any human, divine or demoniac being may be possessed of it (*the ability to create a tulpa*). The only difference comes from the degree of power, and this depends on the strength of the concentration and the quality of the mind itself."

The reason for including this concept here is that one of the problems which dowsers can run into is that the existence of such thoughtforms can give conflicting results.

Bear in mind that, according to David-Néel, anyone can make these, then there are going to be circumstances where such thoughtforms are going to be more prevalent. For example, places which were used to hide treasure are more likely to have such things acting to confuse any searcher. Any particular circumstance where a person focused closely on a particular outcome or deliberately set out to form a confusing mental picture will have created a thoughtform.

Whereas a tulpa has physical form and can even be interacted with to a certain degree, most of what a dowser will be interacting with would be purely energetic. The thoughtform created as protection, diversion or camouflage does not have to be particularly strongly defined, but will often prove sufficient to cause problems.

The other way in which thoughtforms can be an issue for dowsers is where several dowsers or other interested parties have been searching for a specific target. Each will have left their own imprint, their thoughtform, behind as to what their interpretation of the situation could have been. Such a mix and muddle of these energetic imprints can cause great confusion for those who come along later. Thus, people involved in looking for lost objects, people or pets will frequently begin with an assumption (conscious or not) about what is likely to have happened. This energetic idea is then transferred to the locality itself and makes it difficult for subsequent dowsers to know which is the earlier thoughtform and which is the actual energetic residue of the target.

As such, it is good practice to go into such situations with no preconceived ideas, as far as is possible, and to try to remove any energetic imprints you may have left behind.

Also, as has been intimated, as one popular saying goes, "Your thoughts are things." While this has been used most frequently to encourage 'positive thinking', it also means that, if your beliefs (q.v.) are strong enough, it is highly likely that they will create events and dowsing results in such a way as to confirm those beliefs. In other words, thoughtforms are likely to provide your dowsing with the results you expect to have based on your beliefs.

This is yet another reason why dowsers would be better served by an air of innocence and openness as well as a strong sense of wonderment whenever they dowse. A willingness to accept new things, new ideas, is part of it. Such a mindset will be far less likely to trip them up with 'false echoes' and, instead, allow them a far greater range of experiences.

Interestingly, the idea of tulpas has now become far more acceptable in that there are many thousands of people who share online communities concerning the growth, development, care and interaction with their own tulpas, which are always considered as internal aspects of consciousness, whether independent or part of the creator's. The concept is real enough. All it takes is focused mental energy.

Therefore, if a dowser, when dowsing about non-physical targets, uses focused mental energy, then how much of what is found is created by the dowser?

～

TREASURE DOWSING

Treasure dowsing is one of the applications of this skill. It has its own obvious attractions to those who are new to dowsing or who wish to try a new application. Most people think of treasure dowsing as revealing some long-lost, buried treasure. While that is an occasional, rare occurrence, the most usual form of treasure dowsing is to locate coins or placer gold deposits. Of course, it is up to the individual dowser to decide what would constitute 'treasure.'

～

TRUTH

One might, at first, think that this is a simple and open subject. After all, the truth is exactly that, isn't it? However, what at first appears to be obvious and straightforward is anything but.

If the test for truth is dowsing for water, then either the water is found at the depth and at the flow rate and purity as dowsed, or it isn't. A simple means of establishing the truth of the dowsing exercise.

But what if that well was not quite sufficient for the intended purpose, but that only became clear later on? What of returning to the same site some time later and dowsing a new site which has an increased flow of water? Why not have found that one the first time? Why wait until later to find it?

Which one was 'the truth'? Both? Neither?

Or, what if you believe that there are always an odd number of spirits accompanying you when you dowse and that they are there to protect you? You can dowse and find them each time. A varying number, but always odd.

One dowser comes along and finds no such spirits. A third dowser finds a varying number, both even and odd, at varying times. What is 'the truth' then? Who is 'right'? Can it be proven and does it really matter?

But what if you have developed a very detailed and well-researched theory which will explain perfectly how dowsing really works? Can you be sure that your 'truth' is available to be found by other dowsers?

'The truth' is a malleable concept depending upon who is perceiving it, how it is perceived and how important it is that the perception fits an existing model.

There may well be a 'Truth' (with a capital 'T') concerning some over-arching concept such as the universe consisting of consciousness only. (And even that is open to interpretation.)

But there is also the truth of one's own experiences. Such experiences will lead one to certain conclusions, building up a truth edifice. But that edifice is personal.

Some dowsers become almost enraged when their version of the truth is questioned. They are usually firmly of the opinion that things are either as they are or not. This dualism (q.v.) in their thinking precludes them from being able to question their own beliefs (q.v.)

Unless target-specific dowsing is the center of the dialog (and even then as noted above, this can be contentious), it is hard to imagine that there could be any consensus as to what is true or not. What happens when dowsing occurs, where a line between reality and imagination and intuition exists (assuming that it does) makes for a huge difficulty in determining any absolutes such as 'truth'.

Nevertheless, dowsers continue to insist that they have discovered a 'truth,' perhaps even *the* Truth but are unable to adequately defend and explain it in the face of determined questioning and examination.

One of the reasons for this 'need' for truth is that there is a hope that if such a thing can be defined and accepted, then dowsing must, of course, be accepted by society and not be forever pressed onto the sidelines. This is a very understandable thing. But, it does tend to overlook that which makes dowsing special and distinct; the combination of logic and rationality and intuition and imagination which all somehow coalesce in the dowser as she experiences dowsing.

If dowsers could accept the specialness of what they do and seek to nurture that, then there might be an over-arching truth of dowsing which could be agreed upon. But, seeking to force it into an existing paradigm of 'truth' in the hope of further acceptance is to deny what dowsing consists of.

It is safer to say that any truth discovered by any dowser is both plural and contingent. It might have different meanings and interpretations and it might depend solely upon the situation at the time, but that is not to decry that it is a truth.

If dowsers could be persuaded that *a* truth is more important to them than *the* truth, they might well be more able to develop self-reliance and self-understanding which, in turn would serve them better in the long run.

In the meantime, allowing that the concept of 'truth' is not fixed and permanent would be hugely useful, amongst dowsers at least!

U

Underground Water

Underground water has long been one of the targets for dowsers (see WATER DOWSING and WATER WITCHING). As a result, it is also the dowsing application most frequently tested by scientists (See SCIENCE AND DOWSING). Although the earliest written descriptions of dowsing was for minerals (see AGRICOLA), water dowsing is probably the most usual association made about dowsing by the general public.

The geology of underground water is not as clearly defined as geology in general, in that it can appear in very narrow areas as thin streams as well as in wide sheets underground.

One of the usual objections to water dowsing is that it is claimed that drilling anywhere will tap into water (See SKEPTICISM). However, there are numerous well-documented examples of professional water dowsers finding water next to a dry hole made by a drilling company.

Underground water is relatively well-documented in terms of large aquifers and underground streams. But the precise nature of movement underground of water, as well as the electro-magnetic affects of this movement are less well known.

It was long thought that there was a limited amount of underground water available. This was the ground water provided by the working of the hydrological cycle as taught in schools. It was due to this concept that much of what dowsers said they dowsed as being accurate underground was scoffed at by hydrologists.

However, recent investigations have opened up another possibility that other water, named primary water due to its origin deep within the earth and its as yet unexplained manufacture, exists in large quantities. Evidence for water has been found at up to 400 miles beneath the surface, which was totally unexpected.

It is possible that there is yet much more to be learned about underground water.

∿

Underwood, Guy

Guy Underwood (1883 - 1964) is important in that he was an early pioneer in what might be now called earth energy (q.v.) dowsing.

He was primarily interested in discovering the reasons for dowsing tools reacting in certain places. As such it was an attempt to provide another theory for dowsing (see THEORIES).

A major aspect of his ideas was that there were detectable (i.e. dowseable) patterns in the earth which were associated with ancient tracks, holy sites and ancient monuments.

For further details about his ideas, the interested reader is directed to Underwood's posthumously published book, *Patterns of the Past*.

∿

Universal Pendulum

The Universal Pendulum probably has more adherents in mainland Europe, especially in France, than in America and the United Kingdom.

This is, no doubt, due to the fact that it was developed by French dowsers in the 1930's. It fits in with the concept of radiesthesia (q.v.)

It consists of a wooden pendulum with various meridians marked out and a thread with specific lengths at which it should be held indicated by beads.

Inside the pendulum there are, apparently, hemispheres which act as magnifiers of the shape's radiating properties.

According to a description of its use (below), it is only tangentially related to dowsing as most what it is capable of, it does by itself!

There are numerous precise and detailed instructions about tuning it, and how to use it for specific purposes. This has led, in turn, to a great deal of mysticism about it and its use which has made it less popular than it might have been. One of these ideas is that of negative green (q.v.).

For a (very brief) idea of its operation and use, the following is from thenewageblog.com, accessed May 27 2015:

"The Universal Pendulum works on the assumption there are 12 chakras (plus and minus Green count as one), instead of the usual 7 . It does not need any mental instructions for use, as it will either detect or send all by itself different radiating energies within its many adjusting possibilities. It does both of its main functions of diagnosis and treatment at the same time, the Universal Pendulum can turn either way to neutralise any excess energies, but generally it turns clockwise to increase and anticlockwise to reduce colour energies."

Although this particular tool is a pendulum, that does not mean that it is a dowsing pendulum. Of course, it is possible to use it as such, but the main purpose of it is to act as a transmitting device rather than as a device to indicate answers to questions.

～

UNIVERSE, **The**

Many of the ideas, past and present, which seek to explain how dowsing works refer either to some force or forces in the universe responsible for the skill or some form of intimate connection with it which the dowser can access.

To take the first idea, if forces exist (See THEORY OF RATES), then they are thought to act equally on everything, including the pendulum and the dowser. Such a concept allows for the pendulum, held by the dowser or merely suspended, to respond to various substances, minerals or even ideas because it is able to sense this energy, either by itself or through the medium of the dowser. Thus the idea that there is something which can be measured in each and every thing in the universe.

As such, this idea of a common and invisible force or forces, allows a picture of affinities, opposites, vitalities and suchlike to be built up through simply measuring what happens when a pendulum or other appropriate tool is used. It is, in effect, turning dowsing into a method of cataloging and classification. What can be made of such results and the ensuing relationships which are revealed is very much up to the individual. But they tend to end up being codified into something which generally is not challenged in detail but accepted as being a 'truth' (q.v.), allowing for gradations of interpretations and for special cases. Such is the result of the Bovis scale (q.v.) or the long pendulum (q.v.) rates.

The second idea, that of some form of intimate connection with the universe in general, is sought as a way of explaining how the answers are arrived at (See THEORIES). This, it can be seen, is an entirely different approach from the first idea. There, the dowser was simply reflecting or allowing existing data to be revealed. What questioning may have occurred would be limited in nature and be focused on the examination of the essence or subtle internal aspects of the experiment.

This second idea, however, opens up a much wider exploration of what may be possible with dowsing. Whereas in the first instance everything can be measured and cataloged, in the second, everything is open to deeper and more varied investigations.

It is this second idea of a connection with the universe which has allowed dowsing to become the expansive and encompassing tool of the modern day. Prior to this concept, dowsing was largely seen as a practical skill (See WATER DOWSING) and the dowser being influenced by such things as demons or electricity. After this, however, an expanded view of the universe began to be considered more seriously.

Interestingly, such a view of the connection between man (the dowser) and the universe began also to more closely echo the esoteric and metaphysical schools of thought concerning man's relationship with the universe. For some early researchers dowsing was seen as being proof positive of such a connection. This idea, although it has faded somewhat into the background of dowsing, still has some reverberations in the ideas of the holographic universe (q.v), the Akashic Records and the like. The only difference really is that this connection is now more widely acknowledged as being a valid concept and science is turned to more frequently for some level of confirmation (See QUANTUM THEORY).

V

Vastu

Vastu (also variously vaastu and vastuu) is the Indian subcontinent's variation of Eastern Feng Shui or Western Baubiol0gie or space clearing (q.v.), in that it concerns itself with the flow of forces acting in, on and around buildings. The full name is usually Vastu Shastra, normally translated as the Science of Architecture.

It is considered to have its origins as far back as somewhere between 3,000 to 6,000 B.C. and is based on the many very old manuscripts dealing with the subject.

~

Vilsbiburg

Vilsbiburg is a town on the river Große Vils, 18 km southeast of Landshut, in the district of Landshut, in Bavaria, Germany. It was chosen by Freiherr Gustav von Pohl (q.v.) to investigate the causes for so many deaths by cancer, despite its small size. It is considered to be the origin of the modern concept and practice of space clearing (q.v.) because of the results obtained.

Virgula Divina

See DIVINING ROD

W

Water Dome

A water dome or blind spring (q.v.) is the term given to underground water (q.v.) which has risen up but is unable to break the surface of the ground as a spring. The water then radiates away in a number of streams at various levels.

Geologists do not believe that such a formation exists and say that it is entirely in the mind of the dowser. However, amongst water dowsers it is generally accepted that to drill into such a dome would be useless as the resulting well would have little water in it; the action of the drilling would release the pressure.

The number of streams radiating from the dome is usually dowsed to be an odd number.

Blind springs or water domes are often associated with ancient sites and churches, leading some dowsers to allege that it is the construction of such paces which 'attracts' such domes to them. However, there are other places where domes are found where such sites do not exist.

~

Water Dowsing

Water dowsing is one of the most well-known applications of the dowsing skill. Another term for a water dowser is a water witcher (See WATER WITCHING). Because water dowsing is one area where the results can be easily verified (is there water in the well or not, and is it at the dowsed depth and flow rate?), it has frequently been used as a means of testing dowsers and the dowsing process.

Before looking at water dowsing in more detail, it is important to point out some of the problems with using water dowsing as a litmus test of dowsing in general and of water dowsing in particular. Firstly, those scientists who have investigated water dowsers have usually done so from a position of negativity in that they have sought to find out what their initial inclinations suggested to them; that dowsing in any form is done by charlatans in order to dupe others. And by discrediting water dowsing they therefore assume that all dowsing is similarly discredited, on the basis that all dowsing must be carried out in the same way, using the same techniques. Proof of water dowsing would not, however, provide proof of map dowsing (q.v.) or health dowsing (q.v.) or its use in animal communication.

Secondly, the nature of dowsing is that the dowser is both the experimenter and the subject of any investigation, as most of what goes on in dowsing is inside the dowser's mind. However, the prevailing scientific paradigm under which dowsing has been investigated in the past emphasizes that there must be something external to the dowser which is measurable by the prevailing instrumentation and which is repeatable (the *sine qua non* of any scientific investigation). To that end, most dowsing experiments are in the form of one or more dowsers being asked to find pipes full of water, and to discover when water is flowing through them and when it is still. The control of the water and the pipes themselves are usually under the control of the experimenter in such a way as to ensure that the double-blind nature of the experiment is not jeopardized.

However, this is not the usual nature of water dowsing and is entirely artificial and therefore not a really valid method of examining any skill. The reason, of course, for approaching the study of water dowsing in this way is the belief that water dowsers are not necessary at all and anyone can drill anywhere and strike water beneath the surface of the earth. Therefore, a controlled environment is necessary.

A more useful and enlightening (and enlightened) approach would be to examine a water dowser at work in the field and make detailed studies of the ground prior to and after any dowsing. Such an approach was, in fact, carried out at the turn of the 19th century by Professor William Barrett over the course of many years. (The results are to be found in *The Credibility Of Dowsing*). The end result turned him from being skeptical to having a belief in the efficacy of some dowsers which could not be explained by any existing scientific paradigm. In other words, dowsing was proved to be effective.

Returning to the main topic itself, water dowsing has a long history. The extent of this history is, of course, impossible to examine, as most water dowsers would have been working quietly in their communities over generations and would have been accepted as a necessary part of each community. It is very much the same now when water dowsers work. They ply their trade successfully in a limited area but do not gain much recognition beyond it.

Successful water dowsers certainly benefit from training and mentoring and much practice. The best water dowsers appear to have a success rate in the high 90%, which is very good indeed. These successful dowsers are also the ones who specialize in that area, which leads to the conclusion that if you want to become a successful dowser in one area, then you must practice often and not assume proficiency from the start.

One interesting aspect of water dowsing is that, sometimes, the same dowser is brought back to the same property later on to find more water. In such cases, they are usually successful. This leads to the interesting idea that they are only capable of finding the amount of water they have been required to find each time, or, they are in some way creating the new water source which did not exist prior to their first exploration (See also BLÉTON, PARAMELLE, TRUTH and ARMY, DOWSING USED BY).

~

WATER WITCHING

Water-witching is a common name for water dowsing (q.v.). It originated in the late 19th century in America, although the term 'water-witch' was apparently in common use prior to that.

Presumably this term derived from the word 'witch' (originating from the Old English 'wicca' - a male sorcerer) and the meaning of conjuring up or causing something to appear (in this case, water) was the most appropriate explanation of a water dowser's skill.

Another possible origin of the term 'witching' could be from 'wican,' an old term meaning 'to bend' (not to be confused with 'wiccan,' the nature-oriented religion).

Yet another opinion offers the idea that the term comes from the preferred use of the wood of the Witch Hazel to dowse for water. However, this can be discounted on the basis that so many dowsers use a wide variety of tools and wood from a wide variety of trees. If the idea of the best tool was solely based on the idea of affinity (like attracts like), then the use of the branch of the willow tree, which requires a good supply of water to grow, would have to have been considered the tool of choice. Yet it has not been adopted as a term. Therefore, the association of witch hazel with water witching is most probably wrong.

What is of interest, however, is that the term is used for male water dowsers, of whom there are far more reports than there are of females. The term water-wizard is so rare as to be considered non-existent. Why the female term is used for males is probably lost in the mists of time, as is also the reason why there are far fewer females practicing this skill.

~

WHOLE BRAIN APPROACH

When speaking of the human brain and how it works, frequent mention is made of the two most obvious aspects; the logical or rational and the intuitive parts and assigning them each to a hemisphere. Taken together, they would constitute the whole brain working together.

One of the more interesting aspects of dowsing is that this appears to be one activity where both of these parts are needed to be active. This does not mean that they are active at the same time, but both parts are required in order to be successful.

So, for the question, the logical, analytical aspect is required (See QUESTIONS). Without this working well, then the questions will be ill-formed and of less worth.

After the question has been formed, then the appropriate mental state (see DOWSING STATE) is necessary.

Often, after the answer has been obtained, the rational aspect needs to be engaged again in order to formulate the next step in the process or investigation and the sequence is repeated.

Too often, dowsers with little or no training ignore or give too little emphasis to one or both of these states of mind.

Sadly, the New Age, with its emphasis on everything being connected and everything being divine, has devalued critical thinking to a degree amongst certain of its followers. This means that rationality has often long since departed when a new idea is embraced.

It should be emphasized repeatedly that dowsing is a combination of the rational and the intuitive and that both are essential. Giving bias to one without the other is denying oneself access to the full spectrum of what dowsing has to offer.

Also, if nothing else, then this engagement of the two aspects carries with it the benefit of allowing intuition into daily life. As both are used in dowsing, the dedicated dowser will benefit from increased mental and intuitive capabilities.

Using the whole brain is something which is often encouraged by self-help gurus in one way or another. But dowsing appears to be the one activity where such a thing is not only possible, but mandatory, if success is to be had.

∼

WITNESS

A witness is usually considered to be a physical sample of what is being dowsed for. Thus, someone who wants to dowse for oil might have a small phial of the type of oil being sought held in the hand while dowsing. Someone else might dowse for silver or gold while holding a witness of a silver coin or gold ring. Dowsing to locate a person, one might use a spot of blood, a hair or an item of clothing. The term 'witness' is used presumably because the object held by the dower is witnessing, or responding, to the similarity existing between itself and the target.

The theory behind it seems to be that of sympathy. The similar nature of the witness creates a connection (a ray, perhaps, according to some schools of thought) which the dowser then is more easily able to follow to the target (See RAYS OF UNION and FUNDAMENTAL BEAMS).

(The concept of a witness would seem to be an echo of something similar to Plato's theory of forms, where the universal idea of each object is the essence of the object. Thus, all chairs share the same form of 'chair.')

In all such cases of physical representations, the idea is that there is some similarity between the witness and the target. That is why a person can be represented by any of the items noted above. It also means that when dowsing for a lost ring, you could use any circular object, for example.

However, the idea of a witness can also be extended to a very clear visual image held in the mind when dowsing. The same principle is involved; that of a representation of the target in one form or another.

While this does seem to have been in use certainly since the late 19th century, there are inherent problems which could arise. For example, assume that you are dowsing to find 18th century pottery in your backyard. You then have as a witness a small blue fragment you found earlier. However, as a witness deals in similarities, you may well discover that your dowsing uncovers a broken coffee mug which you lost last year, a clay drainage pipe, and a blue crayon. Each of those items shares similarities with the witness and, in the course of your dowsing, you might well have skipped over the precise items you were looking for.

Some people will find that this technique works better for them than for others. The reasons why are not clear but are probably due in some fashion to underlying beliefs (q.v.) about the nature of things, even the nature of reality.

As with most practical aspects of dowsing, if it works for you, then it is something worth doing. If it does not work for you, then something else will.

Y

Y-rods

Y-rods are so called from their shape. Water dowsers, especially, used to cut a branch from a tree (the species only matters if that is the belief (q.v.)), such that there were two long, thin branches able to be held. The end which was cut would be pointing in front of the dowser and would react by dipping (or rising) when over the target.

As such, this is one of the oldest tools known (see AGRICOLA) along with a bobber (q.v.).

A modern version can be made from plastic tubing or thin wires fastened in some fashion as to allow them to be bent and held in tension.

Z

Zahoris

Spanish dictionaries define a Zahori as a "Person to whom is attributed the power to discover the hidden, especially underground streams or wells." Or "an insightful person." The Zahoris are mentioned in the 16th and 17th centuries in Spain as having the faculty of seeing what lies beneath the surface of the ground. They were said to be able to discover dead bodies as well as minerals and gems and water. One of the more intriguing aspects of this tribe (assuming it was a distinct ethnic group) was the frequent mention of their red eyes.

The reason they are included in this present work is that their natural skills, if reported accurately, are such that they seemed to be able to naturally achieve what dowsers tend to do, although it was never seen as being the same as dowsing. Possibly this was due to the fact that they used no tools and, from the surviving reports, lived more on the outskirts of society and therefore were seen as of less interest or worth than 'ordinary' citizens.

However, as an aside, there have been some few persons who have also been able to 'see' into the earth and accurately report on and locate underground water. How that occurs is unknown, but there is no reason to assume the reporting of such events was deliberately misleading. It may, in some way, be due to hypersensitivity (q.v.) of a type not usually acknowledged.

PLEASE LEAVE A REVIEW

We would appreciate your leaving a review where you purchased this book, in order to help future readers decide if it will be a good investment for them. Thank you.

RESOURCES

Other Books

We've written over 20 books on dowsing and related subject and invite you to check them out at your favorite online retailer. The best place to start is our course in a book, entitled *Learn Dowsing: Your Natural Psychic Power.*

ABOUT THE AUTHORS

Maggie and Nigel Percy met online in 2000 through their mutual love of dowsing. They spent the next 20+ years serving a global clientele with dowsing and energy clearing methods. During that time, they presented at many conferences, created the online Dowsing World Summit and gave free dowsing training through videos and articles on their websites. They've written over 20 books on dowsing and metaphysical topics and have published fiction using the pen names Maggie McPhee and Andrew Elgin. To see all their books, visit your favorite online retailer.

www.ingramcontent.com/pod-product-compliance
Lightning Source LLC
LaVergne TN
LVHW051232080426
835513LV00016B/1539